MW00378689

Quilting FOR JOY

Barbara Brandeburg
and
Teri Christopherson

Martingale®
& COMPANY

Quilting for Joy
© 2008 by Barbara Brandeburg and Teri Christopherson

That Patchwork Place® is an imprint
of Martingale & Company®.

Martingale & Company
20205 144th Ave. NE
Woodinville, WA 98072-8478 USA
www.martingale-pub.com

Credits

President & CEO ✳ Tom Wierzbicki

Publisher ✳ Jane Hamada

Editorial Director ✳ Mary V. Green

Managing Editor ✳ Tina Cook

Developmental Editor ✳ Karen Costello Soltys

Technical Editor ✳ Laurie Baker

Copy Editor ✳ Durby Peterson

Design Director ✳ Stan Green

Production Manager ✳ Regina Girard

Illustrator ✳ Robin Strobel

Cover & Text Designer ✳ Regina Girard

Photographer ✳ Brent Kane

Printed in China
13 12 11 10 09 08   8 7 6 5 4 3 2 1

Library of Congress Cataloging-in-Publication Data
Library of Congress Control Number: 2008020940

ISBN: 978-1-56477-849-9

Mission Statement

*Dedicated to providing quality products
and service to inspire creativity.*

Contents

Introduction

Why do we quilt?

Our great grandmothers quilted to put something warm on the bed and use up leftover fabric scraps. But today, we can drive to the nearest strip mall and select from a dizzying array of quilts, blankets, and comforters in dozens of colors. And we don't make our quilts out of old skirts and aprons; we buy yards and yards of high-quality fabrics that—admit it—often end up unused and buried in our fabric stash.

So why do we quilt? Because it's fun! There's just something exciting about handling beautiful fabrics and imagining what they could become. We see a quilt pattern and immediately wonder what it would look like done in a different color or if we changed the border or made it larger for a bed. We arrange blocks on our design wall and move them around until they look just right. We spread out favorite fabrics to admire them, but feel an odd reluctance to cut into them.

It occurred to us recently that there are few practical reasons to sew these days. It's cheaper to buy Halloween costumes at a chain store. It's easier to try on a dress and return it to the rack if it doesn't fit properly. It's faster to buy curtains and decorative pillows at a discount store. But it's not nearly as much fun!

Today, we sew and quilt for the sheer joy of the experience. The finished project may have a purpose—a wedding gift or a holiday table runner—but it's the creative process itself that excites us. We keep on planning projects, buying fabric, and taking classes because it's so rewarding.

We've created these quilts to symbolize the things that bring us joy—family, friends, holidays, nature—and yes, let us quilt just for the sake of quilting. We hope you enjoy these projects as much as we do, and we hope women around the world will continue to sew just for the fun of it.

Barbara Brandeburg and Teri Christopherson

Quiltmaking Basics

We've always believed that quilting should be more about fun than perfection, but following a few basic rules will improve your odds of success. Here are some quilting techniques that have worked well for us.

Selecting and Preparing Your Fabrics

Use only high-quality, 100%-cotton fabrics for quilting. Cotton fabrics hold their shape and are easy to handle, while blends are sometimes difficult to sew and press accurately.

Yardage Requirements

Quantities for all quilts in this book are based on 42"-wide fabrics. We assume at least 40" of usable width after preshrinking, and we specify a minimum width only for a few quilts where it's truly critical.

Preparing Fabric for Quilting

Always prewash fabrics to preshrink and test for color-fastness. Never be tempted to skip this step, no matter how eager you are to start cutting those gorgeous fabrics.

Dark colors, bright colors, and light colors should be washed separately. Reds are especially prone to bleed and may require several washings. You can add a cup of vinegar to the cold rinse water to cure bleeding in some fabrics, or ask the staff at your local quilt store to recommend a product that helps set colors. Don't skimp—wash and rinse until you're certain all the dyes are set, or if still in doubt, replace the fabric with another.

Press your prewashed fabrics, whether yardage or scraps from your stash, before you begin cutting.

Materials and Supplies

Sewing machine. You'll need a reliable machine with a good, sturdy straight stitch for piecing. If it has a programmable blanket stitch and other decorative stitches, appliquéing will be much easier. For machine quilting, a walking foot or darning foot is a must.

Rotary-cutting tools. Nothing makes patchwork go faster than the right cutting tools. Use a rotary cutter and cutting mat plus clear acrylic rulers in commonly used sizes. (Rulers sized 6" x 6", 6" x 24", and 12" x 12" will get you started.)

Needles. For machine piecing and appliqué, a size 70/10 or 80/12 needle works well. If you choose a heavier-weight thread for the appliqué, use a machine embroidery needle.

Pins. Straight pins with glass or plastic heads are easy to handle and easy to keep track of while you're working. Silk pins are a little more expensive, but they're exceptionally thin and can slide through fabric easily. If you use safety pins to baste your quilt layers together, be sure they are rustproof. If you are interrupted and don't get to the quilting right away, you don't want to find that humidity has caused the safety pins to rust and ruin your project.

Threads. Use high-quality mercerized cotton thread for piecing, appliqué, and quilting. Save those bargain-table poly-cotton threads for basting.

Batting. Teri prefers a batting with an 80%-cotton/20%-polyester blend because it has a little more loft but still gives a traditional look and feel. She likes to wash her finished quilts in the washer to remove markings and then dry them on a warm setting in the dryer to shrink the batting, resulting in a slightly wrinkled quilt with a vintage look. Barbara uses a 100%-cotton batting for traditional and wall quilts, featherweight polyester for summer quilts, and low- or medium-loft polyester or cotton-poly blend for all other quilts.

Scissors and seam rippers. You'll need a really good pair of scissors for cutting fabric only. Use another, cheaper pair for cutting template plastic, paper, and cardboard. Keep a small pair of embroidery scissors with sharp blades close by your work area for snipping threads. A seam ripper will come in handy, too—no one can piece hundreds of blocks without a single mistake!

Template plastic. Use sheets of clear or frosted plastic (available at quilt shops) to make durable, accurate templates.

Fusible web. This iron-on adhesive product makes any fabric fusible. Refer to the manufacturer's instructions when applying fusible web to your fabrics. For more information, refer to "Using Fusible Web" on page 7.

Marking utensils. When it's time to mark a quilt top, Teri uses a water-soluble fabric marker, which washes out easily with water. Barbara prefers using white pencils on medium and dark fabrics, and a regular pencil on light fabrics. Whatever you use, test it first on scraps of fabric to make sure the marks can be removed easily when the time arrives. Ask the staff at your local quilt shop for recommendations.

Rotary Cutting

A great time saver, rotary cutting also makes precision cutting easier. We'll give just a brief overview here.

1. Match selvages and align crosswise and lengthwise grains as much as you can. Place the fabric on the cutting mat with the folded edge next to you. Place a square ruler on the fold, and then place a long ruler to its left. The long ruler should just cover the raw edges of the fabric.

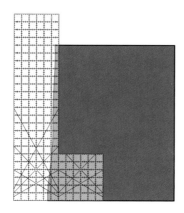

2. Remove the square ruler so that you can cut along the right edge of the long ruler. Always roll the rotary cutter away from you. Discard the uneven scrap.

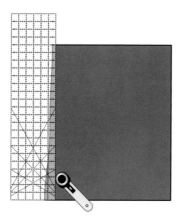

3. To cut strips, align the ruler mark for the required strip width with the fabric edges just squared. Cut along the ruler's edge, rolling the tool toward the selvages.

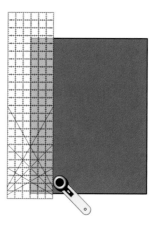

4. To crosscut strips into squares, align the ruler mark for the required measurement with the left edge of the strip. Cut along the ruler's edge. Move the ruler, align it again for the required measurement, and repeat until you have the number of squares needed.

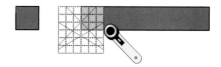

Piecing

All cutting instructions in this book include ¼" seam allowances in the measurements for patchwork, blocks, and borders—every piece except appliqués. It is vitally important to maintain an accurate ¼" seam allowance. If 5 blocks are different in size from the other 25 blocks, they won't fit together correctly. If the blocks are all the same size but the size is incorrect, then sashes, borders, and other pieces won't fit properly. We piece by machine, but if you piece by hand, mark a light guideline for seams on the fabric and keep a ruler by your side for checking accuracy.

Assembly-Line Machine Piecing

To piece by machine, first establish a seam guide exactly ¼" wide. Your machine may have a special foot that measures ¼" from the center needle position to the edge of the foot. Otherwise, create a seam guide by placing a length of tape or moleskin ¼" from the needle as shown.

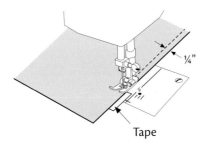

Tape

The fastest way to piece a large number of blocks is to match up identical pieces to be joined at one time. This is often called chain piecing, but we call it assembly-line piecing.

1. Set your machine for 12 stitches per inch. Place the first two fabric pieces to be joined under the needle and sew from edge to edge. Stop at the end of the seam, but do not cut the thread.

2. Feed the next two fabric pieces under the presser foot, sew from edge to edge, and stop. Feed the next two pieces, and so on, without cutting the thread. All seam ends will eventually be crossed by another seam, so there is no need to lock your stitches.

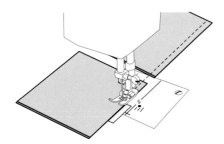

3. When all identical pieces have been stitched, clip the threads to separate them.

Pressing

In quiltmaking, press every seam you sew. The general rule is to press seam allowances to one side, usually toward the darker color. We will occasionally tell you to press seam allowances open because several layers create too much bulk. Unless the instructions specify otherwise, press all seam allowances flat from the wrong side, and then press them in one direction from the

right side. Be careful not to pull or stretch the pieces when pressing.

Appliqué

We use fusible web for the appliqué in our projects. The technique is easy and allows us to work quickly. We trace the patterns onto fusible web, iron them to the wrong side of the fabric, cut out the pieces, peel off the paper, and position the pieces. Then we sew over all the edges with a hand or machine blanket stitch or embroidery stitch, keeping the stitches close together so that the quilts will be washable.

Because we use fusible web, the appliqué patterns in this book are reversed from how they will appear in the quilt and do not include seam allowances. If you appliqué by hand without fusible web, you will need to reverse the templates and add seam allowances.

Making a Template

Use clear or frosted template plastic for durable, accurate templates. Place the template plastic over the pattern and trace with a fine-point permanent marker. Cut out along the lines and mark the piece name and grain line (if applicable).

Using Fusible Web

Use a good-quality, paper-backed fusible web product. There are many brands on the market; if you haven't already found one that you like, ask the staff at your local quilt shop to recommend a lightweight web for the fabrics you're using.

Note: We've calculated the amount of fusible web needed for each project based on a 17" width. Some products come in 12" or 20" widths as well, so purchase accordingly.

Manufacturers' instructions vary for different fusible web products, but here are some general steps to follow. Try it—it's easy and fast and it produces a beautiful quilt. You might never appliqué by hand again.

1. Trace the pattern outline onto the paper side of the web, repeating for as many pieces as are needed from one fabric. (If you need 16 red flowers, trace 16 flowers onto fusible web.) Cut out the shapes,

leaving approximately a ¼" margin all around (not a seam allowance—you'll trim this off in step 3).

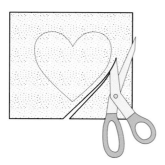

2. Fusible web can make medium and large appliqué shapes too stiff. To prevent this, after tracing the pattern to fusible web, cut out the center of the paper shape, leaving ¼" of paper inside the drawn line. This leaves ¼" of adhesive around the appliqué edge, but the center of the shape will be free of adhesive.

Cut out center
of paper shape.

3. Fuse all the web shapes to the wrong side of the fabric by pressing.

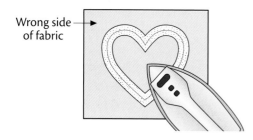

Wrong side
of fabric

4. Carefully cut along the traced lines.

5. Remove the paper backing only when you are ready to fuse the appliqué to the background. Position the appliqué, web side down, on the background fabric and press, following the manufacturer's instructions.

Right side of
background fabric

Right side
of appliqué

6. Stitch around all raw edges except those that will be enclosed in a seam later. This ensures that your quilts will survive washing. We usually use a machine blanket stitch, selecting matching thread for a subtle effect or contrasting thread for a folk-art effect.

Assembling a Quilt Top

Always take the time to measure and square up completed blocks before assembling them in rows. Use a large square ruler to ensure that the blocks are all the same size and that they are actually the designated finished size plus ½" (to allow for a ¼" seam allowance on all sides). If there are variations in size among your blocks, trim the largest to match the smallest. Be sure to square them by trimming all four sides, not just one side.

Sewing Blocks Together

Before sewing your blocks together, arrange them on the floor or a design wall. If the blocks are not identical, move them around until the busiest blocks are evenly balanced across the quilt. When block position is important, we like to number the blocks, writing in the seam allowance with a water-soluble fabric marker or fine-point permanent marker so that we don't forget placement as we sew them together.

1. Sew the blocks together into horizontal rows first. Press the seam allowances according to the project instructions and the pressing arrows shown in the

illustrations. If no specific instructions are given, press the seam allowances in row 1 in one direction, in row 2 in the opposite direction, and so on. Alternating the direction from row to row reduces bulk where seams meet.

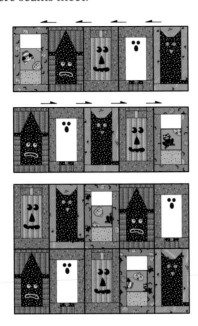

2. Sew the rows together, usually working from the top to the bottom of the quilt. Match all block seams carefully for vertical alignment. Follow the same steps if you're using sashing to join horizontal rows of blocks, alternating row 1, sashing strip, row 2, sashing strip, and so on.

Adding Borders

To avoid wavy borders, we cut our border strips to fit the quilt top. Border measurements are included in the "Assembling the Quilt Top" section of every project. But because quilts don't always come out exactly the size they're supposed to be (especially large quilts), measure your quilt center before you add the borders. If your quilt center turned out smaller, you can trim your borders. If your quilt center turned out larger, you may have to add additional fabric and then cut to fit.

Here's the way we do it:

1. Measure the length of the quilt top through the vertical center. If it deviates more than ½" from the measurement in the instructions, adjust the side-border length before cutting. Cut the side-border strips, piecing as necessary. Mark the centers of

the quilt sides and the border strips. Pin, matching center marks and ends. Sew in place and press.

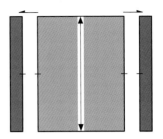

Measure center of
quilt, top to bottom.
Mark centers.

2. Measure the width of the quilt top through the horizontal center, including the side borders. Cut the top and bottom border strips, piecing as necessary. Mark the centers of the quilt and border strips. Pin, matching center marks and ends. Sew in place and press.

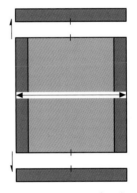

Measure center of quilt,
side to side, including borders.
Mark centers.

Quilting

If you plan to stitch in the ditch or outline quilt a uniform distance from seam lines, it probably isn't necessary to mark the quilting pattern on your quilt top. However, for more complex quilting designs, you'll want to mark the quilt top before assembling the layers.

To be sure you can erase the marks or wash them out, test your fabric marker on a swatch.

Assembling the Layers

Cut your quilt backing 4" to 6" larger than the quilt top. For large quilts, you'll usually have to piece the backing either lengthwise or crosswise. Press the seam allowances open.

1. Spread the backing, wrong side up, on a flat surface. Anchor it with pins or masking tape, being careful not to stretch the backing along the raw edges.

2. Spread the batting over the backing, smoothing out wrinkles.

3. Place the pressed quilt top over the batting, right side up. Make sure the edges are parallel to the edges of the backing fabric.

4. Baste the three layers together. Starting in the center each time, baste diagonally to each corner. Either continue basting in a horizontal and vertical grid, or use rustproof safety pins to hold layers in place. Stitching lines or safety pins should be placed in rows 6" to 8" apart.

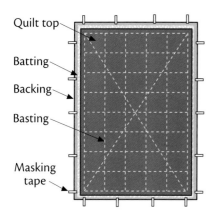

Quilt top
Batting
Backing
Basting
Masking tape

Quilting by Hand

Most quilters use a frame or hoop for hand quilting. Choose the smallest needle you're comfortable using, because it's easier to make small stitches with a small needle. Quilters favor short, sturdy needles called Betweens. Aim for small, evenly spaced stitches, drawn firmly through all three layers.

Quilting by Machine

All our quilts are quilted by machine, and we highly recommend it. It takes much less time than quilting by hand, so you can start another quilt that much sooner.

You'll definitely need a walking foot for straight-line quilting, including stitching in the ditch and outline quilting. This foot is a remarkable help in feeding layers through the machine without shifting or puckering.

Your machine may have a built-in walking foot; if not, the staff at your local sewing-machine store or quilt shop will help you choose the right attachment for your machine.

Walking foot   Quilting in the ditch   Outline quilting

For free-motion quilting, you need a darning foot. Drop the feed dogs on your machine and guide the layers of fabric along your marked design. Use free-motion quilting to stitch around appliqué shapes, to outline quilt a pattern in a print fabric, or to create stippling or curved designs.

 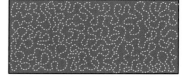

Darning foot   Free-motion quilting

Binding Your Quilt

The binding fabric requirements listed for each quilt in this book are for 2½"-wide strips cut across the width of the fabric as described here.

1. Cut fabric strips 2½" wide. You'll need enough strips to go around the perimeter of your quilt plus 10". Instructions in each project indicate the number of strips you'll need.

2. Sew the strips end to end, right sides together, to make one long piece. Join the strips at right angles and stitch diagonally across the corner. Trim and press the seam allowances open.

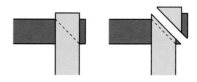

3. Fold the long strip in half lengthwise, with wrong sides together, and press. Cut one end at a 45° angle, turn under ½", and press. You will start sewing with this end. If you haven't already trimmed the backing and batting even with the quilt top, do so now. Also, if you want to add a hanging sleeve (see next section), add it before you bind the edges.

4. Use a precise ¼" seam allowance to attach your binding. Start along one side (not at a corner). Keep raw edges even as you stitch the binding to the quilt top. When you come to the first corner, stop stitching ¼" from the corner and backstitch.

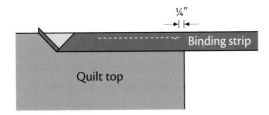

5. Fold the binding up and then back down onto itself, squaring the corner. Turn the quilt 90° under the presser foot. Begin sewing again at the very edge of the quilt top, backstitching to secure the stitches. Continue around the quilt in this manner.

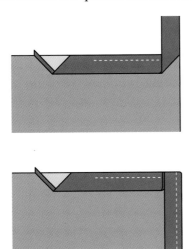

6. When you reach the beginning point, lap the end of the binding over the beginning of the binding, and stitch over the first stitches by 1" to 2". Cut away excess binding and trim the end on the diagonal.

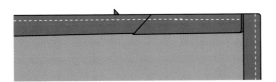

7. Fold the binding over the raw edges of all layers. Use a hand or machine blind stitch to sew the binding to the backing.

Making a Hanging Sleeve

A hanging sleeve is a must for any quilt that will be displayed on a wall. Other methods of hanging put a great deal of stress on the fabrics and will shorten the life of your beautiful quilt considerably.

1. Either use fabrics left over from your quilt or use a length of muslin. Cut a strip 8" wide and about 1" shorter than the width of the top edge of your quilt. Double-fold the short ends (fold under ½", and then ½" again). Stitch down the folded ends.

2. Fold the strip in half lengthwise, wrong sides together, and baste the raw edges to the top edge of the back of the quilt. When you add the binding, the edges of the sleeve will be secured and permanently attached.

3. After your binding is complete, finish the hanging sleeve by blindstitching the bottom folded edge into position as shown.

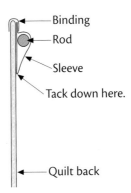

4. Don't forget to sign and date your quilt.

I'm always working on a decorating project, and this year I decided to redo my bedroom the way I did years ago, using my creativity over big spending. It's actually more fun and the outcome is usually better than when you have a grand budget. I cajoled my sister Carol into giving me back an old armchair. It's the ugly, pinky-mauve, striped thing that will never die, but it will look much nicer with a new linen slipcover. I spray painted and distressed the old bedroom set in a black satin finish but updated the look with a new iron bed. This cheery quilt will go on the wall, with white hotel linens on the bed for a newer, trendy style.

We live near Lake Shasta and Mount Shasta, so I got very excited when I discovered the traditional Shasta Daisy block. I think it's fun to give traditional blocks a new twist with current fabrics, colors, or blocks set in a new way. The process of working on a decorating or quilt design project is the fun part for me. As soon as I'm done, I want to start all over again!

Barbara

Materials

Yardage is based on 42"-wide fabric.

14" x 14" scrap *or* 1 fat quarter *each* of 4 blue fabrics, 3 orange fabrics, 3 green fabrics, 2 red fabrics, 2 gray fabrics, 1 yellow fabric, and 1 pink fabric for block backgrounds

8 to 9 fat quarters of assorted white fabrics for daisy appliqués

¾ yard of white fabric for sashing and border

1 fat quarter of yellow fabric for daisy-center appliqués

½ yard of blue fabric for binding

3⅜ yards of fabric for backing

60" x 60" piece of batting

5½ yards of fusible web

Cutting

From *each* of the block background fabrics, cut:

1 square, 12½" x 12½"

From the white fabric for sashing and border, cut:

14 strips, 1½" x width of fabric; crosscut 4 strips into 12 rectangles, 1½" x 12½"

From the blue fabric for binding, cut:

6 binding strips, 2½" x width of fabric

Making the Blocks

1. Refer to "Using Fusible Web" on page 7 and use the patterns on pages 16 and 17 to prepare the appliqués. Make 16 sets of daisies, with each set cut from the same white fat quarter and consisting of one large daisy and four corner daisies. Make 16 large-daisy centers and 64 corner-daisy centers from the yellow fabric.

2. Fold a background square in half and finger-press the fold. Repeat in the opposite direction to mark the block center.

3. Using the daisy appliqués from one set, position the large daisy in the center of the square. Iron to fuse in place. Position a corner daisy in each corner of the square, aligning the raw edges. Iron to fuse in place. Appliqué the edges of each flower using a narrow zigzag stitch and white thread.

4. Position a daisy center on each flower. Iron to fuse in place. Appliqué the edges of each daisy center with a narrow zigzag stitch and yellow thread.

5. Repeat steps 2–4 to make a total of 16 blocks.

Assembling the Quilt Top

1. Referring to the photo on page 15 for color placement, sew four blocks and three white 1½" x 12½" rectangles together as shown. Repeat to make a total of four rows.

Make 4.

2. Sew the 10 white 1½"-wide strips together end to end to make one long piece. From this piece cut five sashing/border strips, 51½" long, and two border strips, 53½" long.

3. Join the rows and three of the 51½"-long strips. Sew the remaining 51½"-long strips to the sides, and then sew the 53½"-long strips to the top and bottom.

Finishing

Refer to "Quiltmaking Basics" on page 5 for detailed instructions on finishing techniques, if needed.

1. Piece the quilt backing so that it is 4" to 6" larger than the quilt top.

2. Layer the quilt top with batting and backing, and baste the layers together.

3. Quilt as desired and use the blue strips to bind using your favorite method.

Finished Quilt Size: 53½" x 53½"
Finished Block Size: 12" x 12"

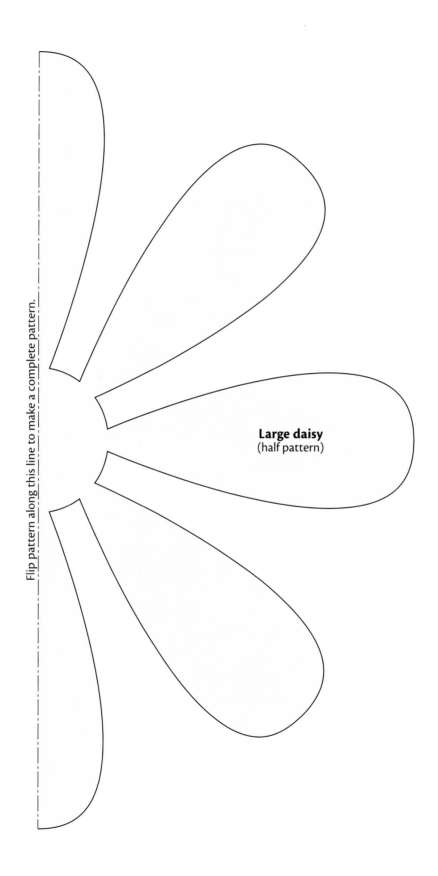

Flip pattern along this line to make a complete pattern.

Large daisy
(half pattern)

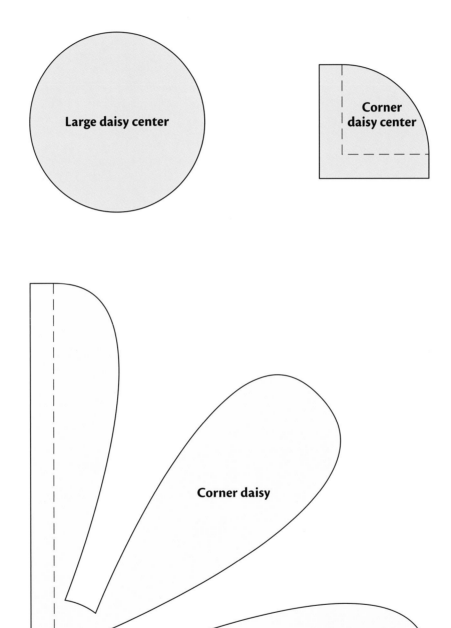

Large daisy center

Corner daisy center

Corner daisy

¼" seam allowance

Baskets Go Round

I love this quilt because it reminds me of my mother. She was unabashedly feminine and loved pretty things. She raised seven children but still managed to keep an elegant living room. With six sisters living there, our house was filled with girl talk—makeup tips, hair advice (whether we wanted it or not), fashion magazines, and midnight gab sessions. We all learned to sew at a young age and spent countless hours at the local fabric shop, picking out fabric for our next outfit.

Now it's cheaper to buy clothes at the mall, but I still love handling beautiful fabric. The gorgeous fabrics in this quilt seemed to leap off the shelf when I saw them. I drafted several ideas before this quilt popped into my head. I love the way the basket handles create a scalloped design. I think my mother would have loved it.

Teri

Materials

Yardage is based on 42"-wide fabric.

2 yards of light floral for setting pieces (do not use a directional print)

2 yards of brown fabric for baskets and binding

1¾ yards of light almost-solid fabric for basket block backgrounds

1½ yards of red floral for border

⅝ yard of red fabric for flowers

½ yard of green fabric for leaves

⅛ yard of yellow fabric for flower centers

4⅝ yards of fabric for backing

73" x 73" piece of batting

1½ yards of fusible web

Cutting

From the light almost-solid fabric, cut:

2 strips, 6⅞" x width of fabric; crosscut into 8 squares, 6⅞" x 6⅞". From the remainder of the strip, cut 8 squares, 2⅞" x 2⅞".

16 strips, 2½" x width of fabric; crosscut into:

16 rectangles, 2½" x 10½"

16 rectangles, 2½" x 8½"

32 rectangles, 2½" x 6½"

From the brown fabric, cut:*

2 strips, 6⅞" x width of fabric; crosscut into 8 squares, 6⅞" x 6⅞". From the remainder of the strip, cut 8 squares, 2⅞" x 2⅞"

3 strips, 2½" x width of fabric; crosscut into 32 squares, 2½" x 2½"

8 binding strips, 2½" x width of fabric

*The remaining brown fabric will be used for basket-handle appliqués.

From the light floral, cut:

1 strip, 20½" x width of fabric; crosscut into 3 rectangles, 10½" x 20½"

1 strip, 10½" x width of fabric; crosscut into 1 rectangle, 10½" x 20½"

1 strip, 15½" x width of fabric; crosscut into 2 squares, 15½" x 15½". Cut the squares in half diagonally in both directions to yield 8 side setting triangles. Pin a label to the triangles so you don't get them mixed up with the triangles cut from the 15" squares.

1 strip, 15" x width of fabric; crosscut into 2 squares, 15" x 15". Cut the squares in half diagonally to yield 4 corner setting triangles. Pin a label to the triangles so you don't get them mixed up with the triangles cut from the 15½" squares.

From the red floral, cut:

7 strips, 6½" x width of fabric

Making the Blocks

1. Use a pencil and ruler to draw a diagonal line on the wrong side of the light almost-solid 6⅞" squares. Place each light almost-solid square with a brown 6⅞" square, right sides together and raw edges even. Sew ¼" away from both sides of the drawn line. Cut on the line. Press the seam allowances toward the brown fabric. You will end up with 16 large triangle-square units.

Make 16.

2. Repeat step 1 with the light almost-solid squares and brown 2⅞" squares to make 16 small triangle-square units.

3. Place a brown 2½" square on a light almost-solid 2½" x 6½" rectangle exactly as shown, right sides together and raw edges even. Sew diagonally across the square as shown. Cut off the outer corner, leaving a ¼" seam allowance. Press the brown triangle back. Repeat to make a total of 16 units. Label them "step 3."

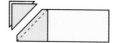

Make 16.

4. Repeat step 3, but place your brown squares on the opposite end of the light almost-solid rectangles and sew across the diagonal as shown. Repeat to make a total of 16 units. Label them "step 4."

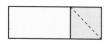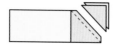

Make 16.

5. Sew a step 3 unit to a large triangle-square unit as shown. Press the seam allowance toward the step 3 unit. Repeat to make a total of 16 units.

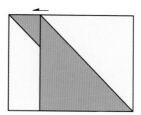

Make 16.

6. Sew a step 4 unit to a small triangle-square unit as shown. Press the seam allowance toward the step 4 unit. Repeat to make a total of 16 units.

Make 16.

7. Sew the step 5 and 6 units together. Add a light almost-solid 2½" x 8½" rectangle to the top of the piece. Sew a light almost-solid 2½" x 10½" rectangle to the right side of the piece. Repeat to make a total of 16 blocks.

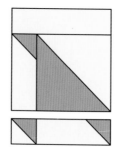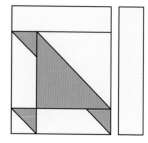

Make 16.

8. Refer to "Using Fusible Web" on page 7 and use the patterns on page 23 to prepare the appliqués. Make 16 basket handles from the remaining brown fabric, 16 flowers from the red fabric, 16 flower centers from the yellow fabric, and 32 leaves from the green fabric.

Finished Quilt Size: 69" x 69"

Finished Block Size: 10" x 10"

9. Refer to the photo on page 21 as needed to apply the appliqué pieces to each block as follows:

   a. Place the basket handle on the block. Iron to fuse in place.

   b. Place the leaves next, but do not iron them yet. Their inner points meet in the center of the block and their outer points should angle downward.

   c. Place the flower and flower center last. One flower petal should point straight up, and the midline petals should overlap the basket slightly.

   d. Iron to fuse the leaves, flower, and flower center in place.

   e. Appliqué the edges of each piece with a narrow machine blanket stitch and matching thread.

Make 16.

Assembling the Quilt Top

1. Sew two blocks together as shown. Repeat to make a total of six pairs.

2. Sew two pairs together to make the center square.

3. Sew the Basket blocks, light floral 10½" x 20½" rectangles, and side and corner setting triangles into diagonal rows. Sew the diagonal rows together to complete the quilt center.

4. Measure the quilt center's width and length in three places—across the center and at both ends. The width and length need to be the same, so determine the average if necessary and write it down.

5. Sew the red floral strips together end to end to make one long piece. From this piece cut two border strips the length determined in step 4 and two border strips the width determined in step 4 plus 12". Sew the shorter strips to the sides of the quilt center and the longer strips to the top and bottom. Press all seam allowances toward the border strips as you add them.

Finishing

Refer to "Quiltmaking Basics" on page 5 for detailed instructions on finishing techniques, if needed.

1. Piece the quilt backing so that it is 4" to 6" larger than the quilt top.

2. Layer the quilt top with batting and backing, and baste the layers together.

3. Quilt as desired and use the remaining brown 2½"-wide strips to bind using your favorite method.

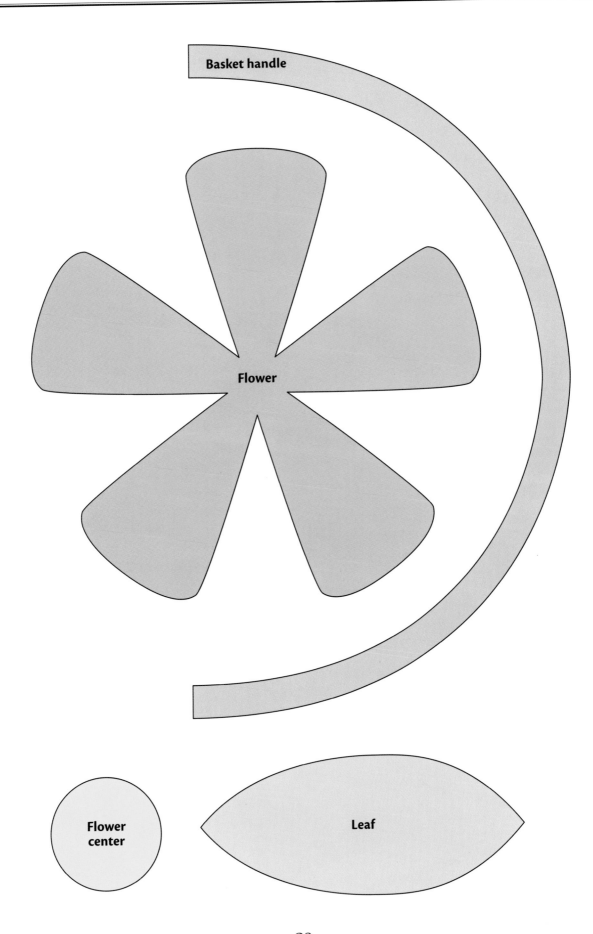

Basket handle

Flower

Flower center

Leaf

Picnic Basket

One of our favorite family experiences is being out in nature. We prefer being in the mountains, fishing on the river, kayaking on the lake, strolling along a stream, or visiting our wonderful national parks. For years we went on an annual camping and fishing trip in northern California. When the boys went fishing, my daughter and I would go berry picking. I took great pride in the berry pies I baked on top of a camp stove in a cardboard box covered in foil.

Now we're making new nature memories with the next generation. No matter where we go, we always seem to take along an old quilt. I prefer a big square quilt that's just perfect for picnics, wrapping up the little ones, or throwing over the lap of someone sitting by the campfire. You just have to have a quilt along for the fun, and this speedy project really fits the bill. I made it to take along on our outdoor adventures with our new little nature lover, grandson Hunter.

Barbara

Materials

Yardage and strips are based on 42"-wide fabric. Rolls of precut 2½"-wide strips are commonly available in quilt shops. Two rolls will provide you with the required amount of strips for this project, although the amount of strips needed in each color for this project may not be the same as those in the roll. You can cut your own strips from standard yardage, if desired. Cut the strips 2½" x 42". Also, if the strips from your roll or yardage are narrower than 42", you will need more strips than the amount listed.

1¾ yards of off-white fabric for block centers, pieced sashing, and pieced border

⅞ yard of black fabric for block centers, pieced sashing, and pieced border

12 assorted red precut 2½"-wide strips for blocks and binding

12 assorted blue precut 2½"-wide strips for blocks and binding

8 assorted green precut 2½"-wide strips for blocks

6 assorted light blue precut 2½"-wide strips for blocks

2 assorted yellow precut 2½"-wide strips for blocks

4 yards of fabric for backing

70" x 70" piece of batting

Cutting

From the black fabric, cut:

3 strips, 2½" x width of fabric; crosscut into 38 squares, 2½" x 2½"

12 strips, 1½" x 26½"

From the off-white fabric, cut:

3 strips, 2½" x width of fabric; crosscut into 34 squares, 2½" x 2½"

24 strips, 2" x 26½"

Making the Black-and-White Units

1. Sew five black and four off-white 2½" squares together to form a nine-patch unit. Press the seam allowances as indicated. Repeat to make a total of four units for the block centers.

Make 4.

2. Sew two black and two off-white 2½" squares together to form a four-patch unit. Press the seam allowances as indicated. Repeat to make a total of nine sashing cornerstone units.

Make 9.

3. Sew a black 1½" x 26½" strip between two off-white 2" x 26½" strips. Press the seam allowances toward the black strip. Repeat to make a total of 12 sashing/border strip sets.

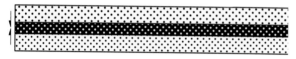

Make 12.

Making the Blocks

1. Sew together six light blue and two yellow precut 2½"-wide strips along the long edges to make a strip set. Press the seam allowances open or to one side. Cut the strip set into four segments, 10½" wide. Repeat with the red, blue, and green precut 2½"-wide strips. Set aside the remaining blue and red strips for the binding.

10½"

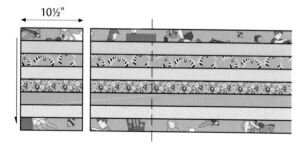

2. Sew a light blue segment to the right side of a nine-patch unit, stopping the seam halfway down the unit. You will complete this portion of the seam later. Press this seam allowance and all the remaining block seam allowances toward the strip-set segments as you go.

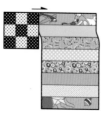

3. Sew the remaining light blue segments to the top of the nine-patch unit, followed by the left side, and

then the bottom of the unit. Sew the unfinished seam from step 2.

 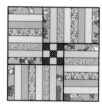

4. Repeat steps 2 and 3 with the red, green, and blue strip-set segments to make one red block, one green block, and one blue block.

Assembling the Quilt Top

1. Join three four-patch units with two sashing/border strip sets. Repeat to make a total of three pieced sashing/border strips.

Make 3.

2. Join three of the remaining border/sashing strip sets and two blocks to make a block row. Press the seam allowances toward the strip sets. Repeat to make a second block row. Join the block rows and the pieced sashing/border strips.

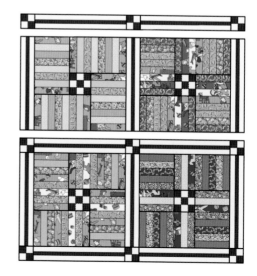

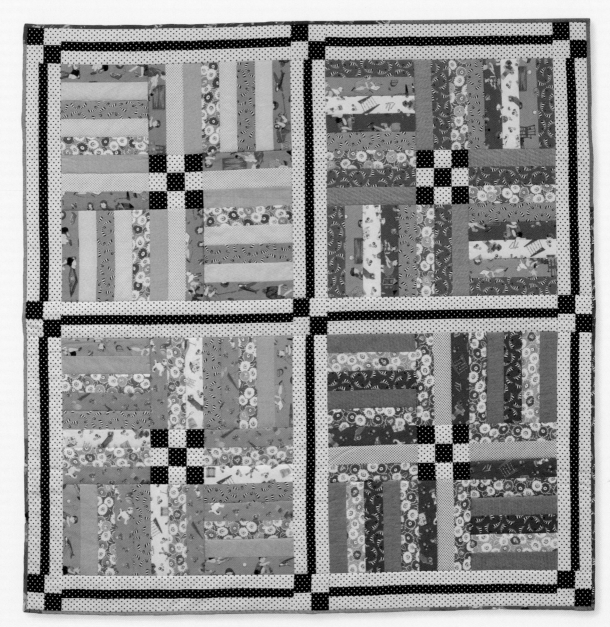

Finished Quilt Size: 64½" x 64½"

Finished Block Size: 26" x 26"

Finishing

Refer to "Quiltmaking Basics" on page 5 for detailed instructions on finishing techniques, if needed.

1. Piece the quilt backing so that it is 4" to 6" larger than your quilt top.

2. Layer the quilt top with batting and backing, and baste the layers together.

3. Quilt as desired.

4. Sew the remaining red precut 2½"-wide strips together end to end. Add the remaining blue precut 2½"-wide strips to the end of the red strips to make a scrappy binding. Attach the binding to your quilt, using your favorite method.

A few years ago, on a whim, we picked up and moved to a new part of California. We wanted to work a little less, live closer to the mountains, and have a little less traffic. The idea of a new adventure was thrilling, especially the idea of making many new friends. The only part that really made me nervous was leaving behind a few kindred-spirit girlfriends. You know the kind—someone who loves fabric and design, gets a thrill over a thrift store find, collects fun little antique treasures, decorates with flair, or gets a kick out of life in the garden.

I was pleasantly surprised to discover that creative gals are everywhere, and we just seem to flock together. One of my favorite new creative friends just moved to a darling little cottage that inspired this cheery, fun pillow. Usually I work out a design with a pencil and paper before I get started, but this time around, I just snipped away at scraps of fabric until it was "just right." I love it when a project makes me happy while I make it, and even more if it gives me a thrill after it's done.

Barbara

Materials

Yardage is based on 42"- wide fabric.

1⅔ yards of white linen fabric for pillow front and back

¼ yard of red fabric for border

Large scrap of gray fabric for pot

Scraps of assorted aqua fabrics for pot band and bird body

Scraps of assorted red fabrics for flowers and berries

Scraps of assorted orange and yellow fabrics for flowers and letters

Scrap of dark brown fabric for flower centers

Scraps of assorted green fabrics for leaves

Scrap of brown fabric for bird legs

Scrap of black fabric for bird eye

⅞ yard of fusible web

20" x 20" pillow form

Cutting

From the fusible web, cut:

1 piece, 5" x 20"

From the white linen fabric, cut:

1 square, 24½" x 24½"

2 rectangles, 14½" x 24½"

Making the Pillow Front

1. Follow the manufacturer's instructions to apply the fusible web piece to the wrong side of the red fabric. From the fused piece, cut four border strips, 1" x 19".

2. On the right side of the white linen 24½" square, center a red strip 2¾" from each side. Position the remaining two border strips 2¾" from the top and bottom edges, overlapping the ends of the side border strips. If desired, trim the ends of the side borders to reduce bulk. Iron to fuse in place. Appliqué the edges with a buttonhole stitch and matching thread.

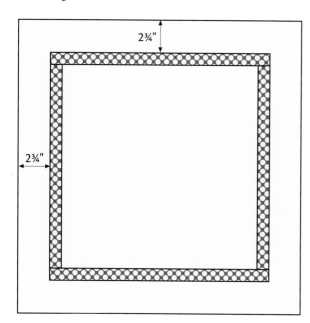

3. Refer to "Using Fusible Web" on page 7 and use the patterns on pages 33–35 to prepare the remaining appliqués. Make each appliqué from the appropriate fabric, referring to the materials list and the photo on page 31. Cut one of *each* shape.

4. Refer to the placement guide at right to apply the appliqué pieces as follows:

   a. Position the pot 1" above the bottom red border, 5" from the left border, and 6" from the right border. Iron to fuse in place.

   b. Position the letters ⅝" to the left of the pot. Iron to fuse in place.

   c. Position the remaining shapes. Iron to fuse in place.

d. Appliqué the edges of each piece with a button-hole stitch in matching thread.

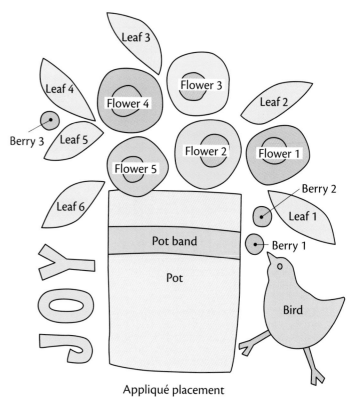

Appliqué placement

Finished Pillow Size: 19" x 19"
plus 2½" flange

Assembling the Pillow

1. To create the pillow back, fold under ¼" on one long edge of each white linen 14½" x 24½" rectangle, and then fold it under ¼" again. Press the hems. Stitch the hems in place with white thread.

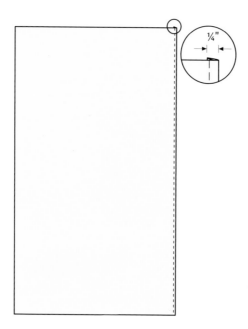

2. With right sides together, pin the pillow back pieces over the pillow front, matching the raw edges. The hemmed edge of the back pieces will overlap a few inches at the center. Sew around the perimeter of the pillow, ¼" from the pillow edges.

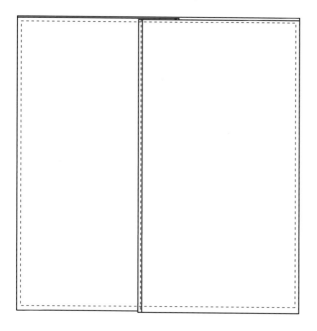

3. Trim across the corners, being careful not to snip the stitching. Turn the pillow cover right side out. Press flat.

4. Using white thread, stitch just outside the red border, through both thicknesses of the front and back pillow cover. Insert the pillow form into the cover. The pillow form is 1" larger than the opening. This is a technique used by professional decorators that will keep your pillow top from sagging.

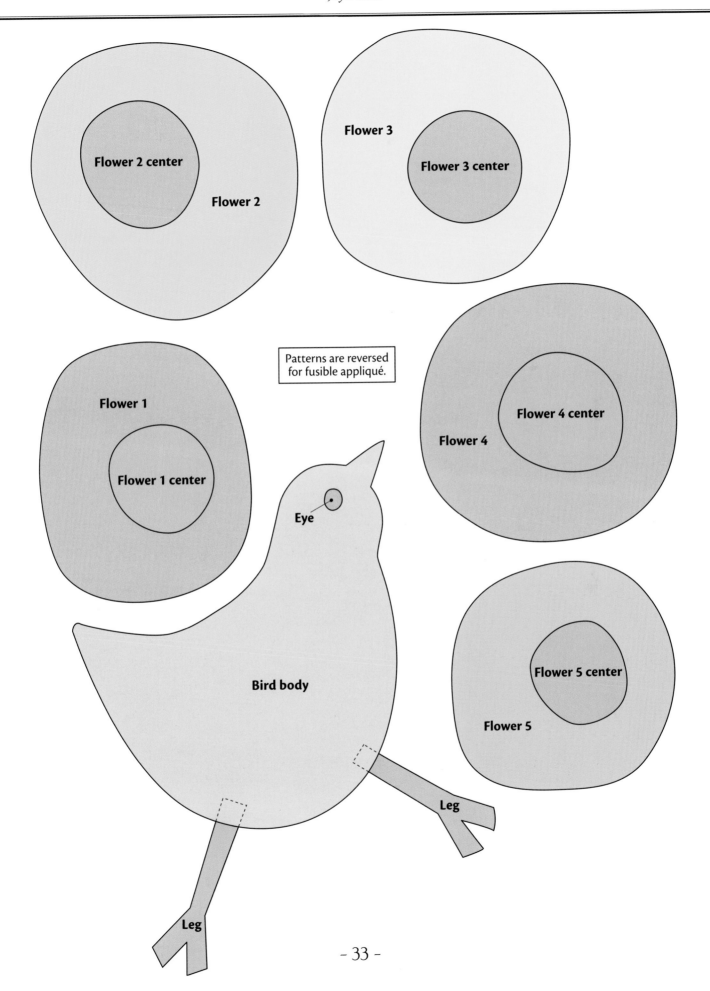

Flower 2 center

Flower 2

Flower 3

Flower 3 center

Patterns are reversed for fusible appliqué.

Flower 1

Flower 1 center

Flower 4 center

Flower 4

Eye

Bird body

Flower 5 center

Flower 5

Leg

Leg

Patterns are reversed
for fusible appliqué.

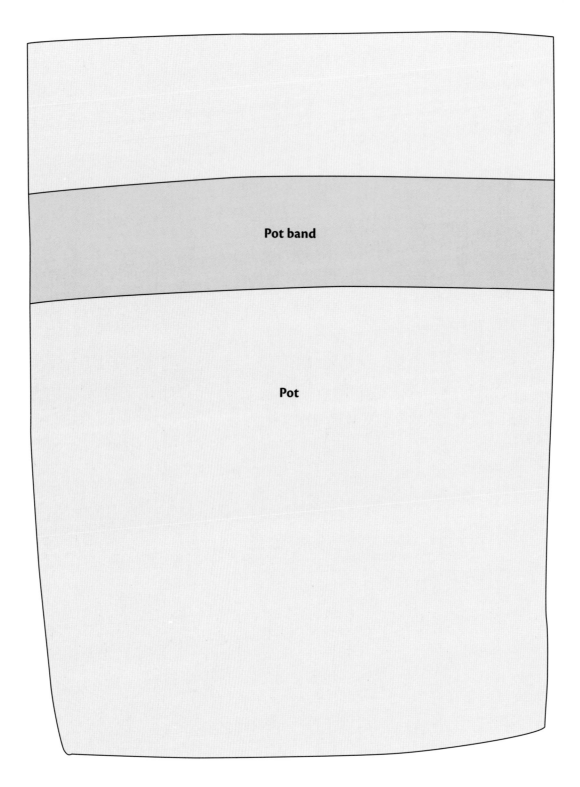

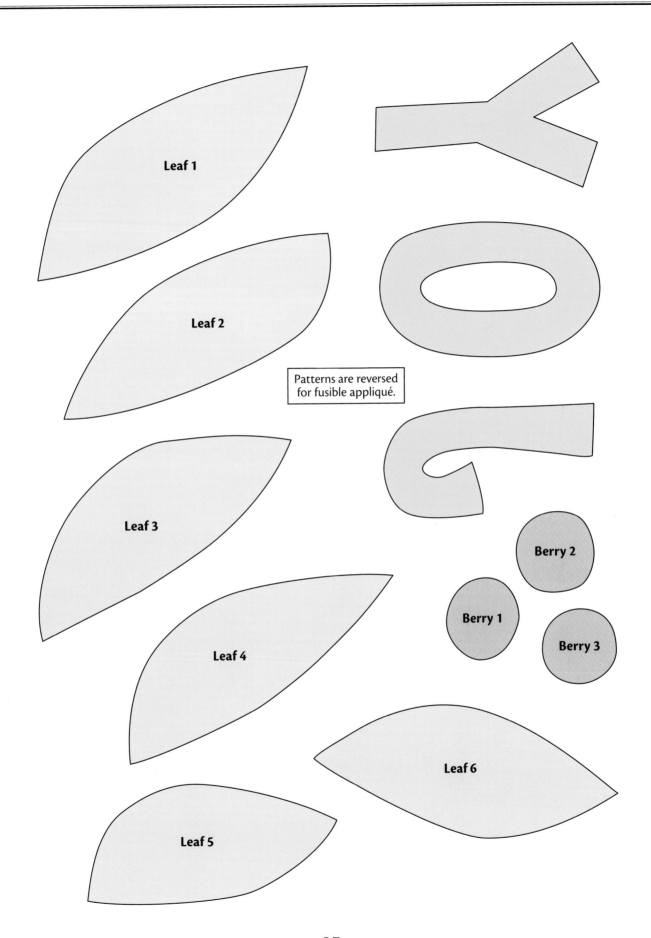

Leaf 1

Leaf 2

Patterns are reversed
for fusible appliqué.

Leaf 3

Berry 2

Leaf 4

Berry 1

Berry 3

Leaf 6

Leaf 5

Matilija Poppies

Few things bring me more joy than the beauties of nature. My home is nestled in the dry, rolling hills of Southern California. Most of the native vegetation is rather scrubby looking, so as I drove along the highway one day I was startled to see a tall shrub covered with enormous, fluttering white flowers, like white handkerchiefs blowing in the breeze. I looked up the plant when I got home and discovered that it was a Matilija poppy, which thrives in our arid climate and explodes with remarkable, six-inch flowers once a year. I got excited about planting one in my backyard, until I learned that they grow over 10' tall, are very picky, very invasive, and very hard to remove. Ah, well, I'll just enjoy them along the highway. I designed this quilt with daisies in mind, but knew as soon as it was finished that they were Matilija poppies.

Teri

Materials

Yardage is based on 42"-wide fabric.

5¼ yards of blue fabric for blocks and borders

2½ yards of ivory fabric for blocks and pieced border

1⅓ yards of yellow fabric for blocks, second border, and binding

5⅝ yards of fabric for backing

70" x 94" piece of batting

Cutting

From the blue fabric, cut:

7 strips, 6½" x width of fabric; crosscut into 38 squares, 6½" x 6½"

10 strips, 2¼" x width of fabric; crosscut into 156 squares, 2¼" x 2¼"

8 strips, 3½" x width of fabric; crosscut into:
    44 rectangles, 3½" x 6½"
    4 squares, 3½" x 3½"

8 strips, 3½" x width of fabric

7 strips, 5½" x width of fabric

From the ivory fabric, cut:

23 strips, 3½" x width of fabric; crosscut into 244 squares, 3½" x 3½"

From the yellow fabric, cut:

7 strips, 1½" x width of fabric

9 binding strips, 2½" x width of fabric

Making the Blocks

1. Place a blue 2¼" square at one corner of an ivory 3½" square, right sides together and raw edges even. Sew diagonally across the blue square as shown. Cut off the outer corner, leaving a ¼" seam allowance. Press the blue triangle back. Repeat to make a total of 156 units. (You will have 88 ivory squares left over.)

Make 156.

2. Sew together two units exactly as shown on the left. Press the seam allowance in the direction shown. Repeat to make a total of 48 pairs. Sew together two units exactly as shown on the right. Press the seam allowance in the direction shown. Repeat to make a total of 30 pairs. Be sure to keep your two stacks separate.

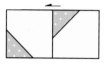 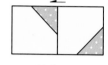

Make 48. Make 30.

3. Sew together two of the pairs from the left-hand stack as shown to make Poppy block A. Repeat to make 24 blocks. Sew together two of the pairs from the right-hand stack as shown to make Poppy block B. Repeat to make 15 blocks. Be sure to keep your two stacks of blocks separate. Refer to "Using Fusible Web" on page 7 and use the pattern on page 40 to prepare 39 yellow flower centers for appliqué. Position an appliqué in the center of each block. Iron to fuse in place. Appliqué the edges of the circles with a narrow machine blanket stitch and matching thread.

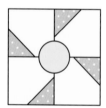 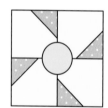

Block A. Block B.
Make 24. Make 15.

4. Use a sharp pencil and ruler to draw a line across the diagonal on the wrong side of the 88 remaining ivory 3½" squares. Place an ivory square at one end of a blue 3½" x 6½" rectangle, right sides together and raw edges even. Sew on the drawn line. Cut off the outer corner, leaving a ¼" seam allowance. Press the ivory triangle back. Repeat on the opposite end

to create a Flying Geese block. Repeat to make a total of 44 blocks.

 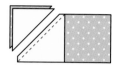

 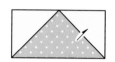

Make 44.

Assembling the Quilt Top

1. Alternately sew together four A blocks and three blue 6½" squares. Press the seam allowances toward the blue squares. Repeat to make a total of six rows.

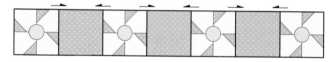

Make 6.

2. Alternately sew together three B blocks and four blue 6½" squares. Press the seam allowances toward the blue squares. Repeat to make a total of five rows.

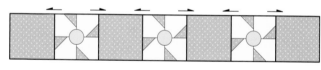

Make 5.

3. Refer to the quilt assembly diagram on page 41 to sew the rows together, alternating the A and B block rows, to complete the quilt center.

4. Sew the blue 5½"-wide strips together end to end to make one long piece. From this piece, cut two border strips, 66½" long, and two border strips, 52½" long. Sew the 66½"-long strips to the sides of the quilt, and then sew the 52½"-long strips to the top and bottom of the quilt.

Finished Quilt Size: 66½" x 90½"

Finished Poppy Block Size: 6" x 6"

Finished Flying Geese Block Size: 3" x 6"

5. Sew the yellow 1½"-wide strips together end to end to make one long piece. From this piece, cut two border strips, 76½" long, and two border strips, 54½" long. Sew the 76½"-long strips to the sides of the quilt, and then sew the 54½"-long strips to the top and bottom of the quilt.

6. With the blue points facing the same direction, sew together nine Flying Geese blocks end to end. Add a blue 3½" square to the ends of the strip. Repeat to make a total of two top/bottom borders. Sew together 13 Flying Geese blocks end to end. Repeat to make a total of two side borders. Sew the Flying Geese side borders to the sides of the quilt, making sure the blue points are facing the quilt center. Sew the Flying Geese top/bottom borders to the top and bottom of the quilt in the same manner.

7. Sew the eight remaining blue 3½"-wide strips together end to end to make one long piece. From this piece, cut two border strips, 84½" long, and two border strips, 66½" long. Sew the 84½"-long strips to the sides of the quilt, and then sew the 66½"-long strips to the top and bottom of the quilt.

Finishing

Refer to "Quiltmaking Basics" on page 5 for detailed instructions on finishing techniques, if needed.

1. Piece the quilt backing so that it is 4" to 6" larger than your quilt top.

2. Layer the quilt top with batting and backing, and baste the layers together.

3. Quilt as desired and use the yellow strips to bind using your favorite method.

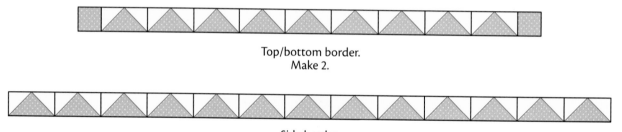

Top/bottom border.
Make 2.

Side border.
Make 2.

Flower center

Quilt assembly

Flowers for Debbie

Quilting isn't just fun; it can also be healing. My friend Debbie is one of the most beautiful women I've ever known, both inside and out, and I was so worried when I learned she'd been diagnosed with breast cancer. She called one afternoon to ask if I had any quilt kits lying around the house. She was going to be stuck at home for a few months and wanted a hand-sewing project. I didn't have any kits but was so glad she'd called, so I could help in some small way. She said her favorite color was red, and she wanted a project with flowers in it to symbolize springtime and renewal. "It will keep my hands busy, and when this challenging time is over, I'll have something lovely to take away from it." Leave it to Debbie to find a silver lining!

I spent a couple of days preparing appliqué blocks, then drove over and taught her to do a hand blanket stitch. A few weeks later, she called to announce, "I'm finished! I couldn't stop sewing. I love it!" Her quilt turned out so beautifully, I made a second one for myself, shown here. I'm happy to report that Debbie is now cancer free and taking hand-appliqué classes.

Teri

Materials

Yardage is based on 42"-wide fabric.

4 yards of red toile fabric for sashing and middle border

2⅛ yards of light print for appliqué block backgrounds and sashing cornerstones

1½ yards of green fabric for inner border, outer border, and binding

1¼ yards of golden tan fabric for baskets

⅝ yard *total* of assorted green fabrics for leaves

⅜ yard *total* of assorted red fabrics for flowers and flower centers

¼ yard *total* of assorted yellow fabrics for flower centers

6¾ yards of fabric for backing

76" x 104" piece of batting

3½ yards of fusible web

Water-soluble fabric marker

Cutting

From the light print, cut:

5 strips, 11½" x width of fabric; crosscut into 15 squares, 11½" x 11½"

3 strips, 3½" x width of fabric; crosscut into 24 squares, 3½" x 3½"

From the red toile fabric, cut:

13 strips, 3½" x width of fabric; crosscut into 38 rectangles, 3½" x 11½"

8 strips, 10½" x width of fabric

From the green fabric for borders and binding, cut:

15 strips, 1½" x width of fabric

9 binding strips, 2½" x width of fabric

Making the Blocks

1. Refer to "Using Fusible Web" on page 7 and use the patterns on page 47 to prepare the appliqués. Make 15 baskets from the golden tan fabric, 15 large flowers and matching flower centers from the assorted red fabrics, 15 small flowers from the assorted yellow fabrics, and 90 leaves from the assorted green fabrics. To reduce bulk, cut out the center of the fusible web paper shapes before ironing them to the wrong side of the fabrics.

2. To help position the appliqués, draw placement lines on the right side of the 11½" light print squares with the water-soluble fabric marker. Draw one vertical line down the center of the square, one horizontal line across the center of the square, and two short cross lines across the horizontal line, 1½" from the center of the square.

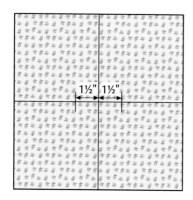

3. Place the appliqué pieces on the squares. Position the basket first, aligning the center of the basket with the horizontal placement line. Iron to fuse in place. Position the four angled leaves next, positioning their inner points at the short cross lines. Keep their points a smidgen away from one another to prevent overcrowding. Do not iron them down yet; wait until all the remaining pieces are positioned.

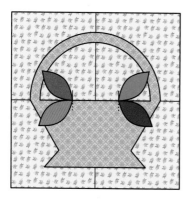

4. Place the two center leaves next, positioning their *outer* points so they just touch the basket's outer edge. Do not worry about their inner points; the outer points are more important. Place the large flower and then the small flower on the block, rotating the red flower so its petals are equally divided by the vertical placement line. Center the flower center appliqué that matches the large flower on the small flower. Iron to fuse in place. Appliqué the edges of each shape with a blanket stitch and matching thread.

Make 15.

Assembling the Quilt Top

1. If your flowers are scrappy like mine, lay out the blocks on the floor in five rows of three blocks each. Move the blocks around until the brightest and busiest fabrics are evenly distributed across the quilt. To remember placement, use the water-soluble fabric marker to write 1–15 on the blocks or pin paper labels onto them.

2. Alternately sew together four red toile 3½" x 11½" rectangles and three blocks. Press the seam allowances toward the red toile. Repeat to make a total of five block rows.

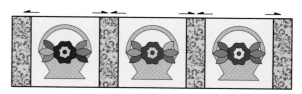

Make 5.

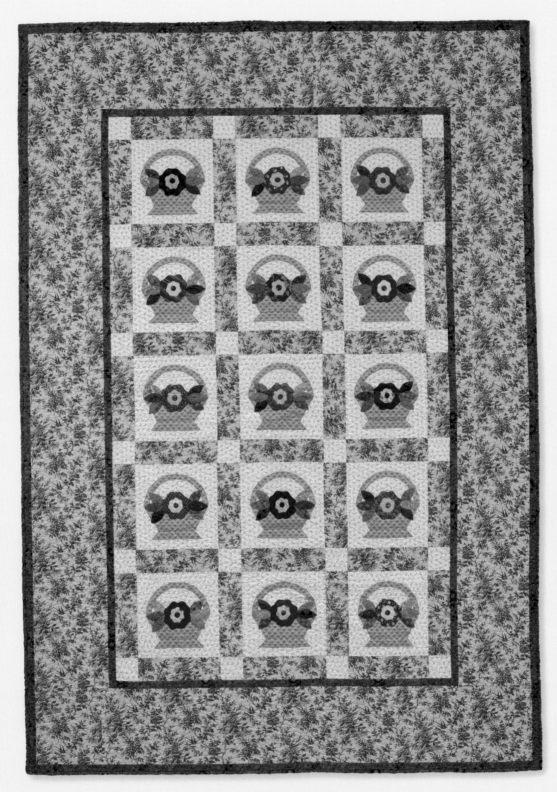

Finished Quilt Size: 69½" x 97½"

Finished Block Size: 11" x 11"

3. Alternately sew together four light print 3½" squares and three red toile 3½" x 11½" rectangles. Press the seam allowances toward the red toile. Repeat to make a total of six sashing rows.

Make 6.

4. Sew the rows together, alternating the sashing rows and block rows, to make the quilt center. Press the seam allowances toward the sashing rows.

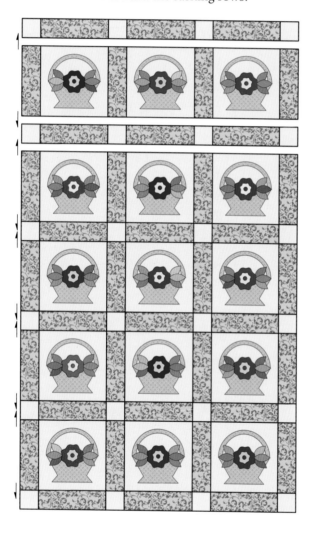

5. Sew the green 1½"-wide strips together end to end to make one long piece. From this piece, cut two border strips, 73½" long, two border strips, 47½" long, two border strips, 95½" long, and two border strips, 69½" long. Sew the 73½"-long strips to the sides of the quilt, and then sew the 47½"-long strips to the top and bottom of the quilt. Set aside the remaining strips for the outer border.

6. Sew the red toile 10½"-wide strips together end to end to make one long piece. From this piece, cut two border strips, 75½" long, and two border strips, 67½" long. Sew the 75½"-long strips to the sides of the quilt, and then sew the 67½"-long strips to the top and bottom of the quilt.

7. Sew the green 95½"-long strips to the sides of the quilt, and then sew the green 69½"-long strips to the top and bottom of the quilt.

Finishing

Refer to "Quiltmaking Basics" on page 5 for detailed instructions on finishing techniques, if needed.

1. Piece the quilt backing so that it is 4" to 6" larger than your quilt top.

2. Layer the quilt top with batting and backing, and baste the layers together.

3. Quilt as desired and use the green strips to bind using your favorite method.

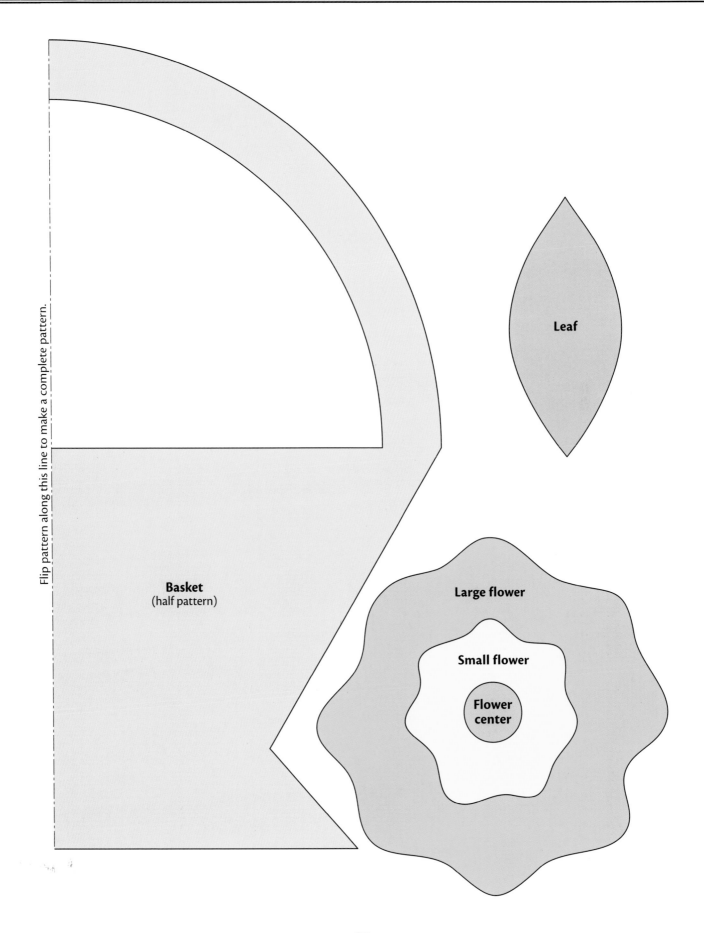

Flip pattern along this line to make a complete pattern.

Basket
(half pattern)

Leaf

Large flower

Small flower

Flower center

One of my favorite things to do is to create a new project while watching a DVD alone in my studio. My favorite movies are the type with historical costumes, artful photography, and wonderful music. Jane Austin and love stories come to mind! I kind of go into a creative trance or zone that is often referred to as "flow." Time disappears and I just feel so joyful and fulfilled while snipping away or chain piecing my little triangles or scraps. How do you explain this to someone who doesn't quite understand the relaxing joy that comes while cutting perfectly fine fabric into hundreds of little pieces and then carefully sewing them all back together again?

I was looking for a circle template one night while trying my hand at yo-yos, and I saw one of my DVDs on the counter. "Hmmm. What about doing a new kind of yo-yo?" I thought. I popped a movie into the DVD player and got to work. This ended up being a perfect movie project. It uses the kind of repetition that doesn't require a lot of concentration, so you can keep your mind on the plot and your eye on the visual beauty of the movie. I did most of the cutting for this quilt while sitting on the floor in front of the couch, watching *Pride and Prejudice.*

Barbara

Materials

Yardage is based on 42"-wide fabric.

3⅜ yards of red fabric for block backgrounds and binding

12 fat quarters of assorted fabrics for circles (I used 5 white or light prints, 3 green prints, 2 yellow prints, 1 brown print, and 1 blue print)

3 yards of fabric for backing

51" x 66" piece of batting

2⅞ yards of lightweight nonwoven fusible interfacing

Cutting

From the interfacing, cut:

108 squares, 5½" x 5½"

From the fat quarters, cut a *total* of:

108 squares, 5½" x 5½"

From the red fabric, cut:

12 squares, 15¼" x 15¼"

6 binding strips, 2½" x width of fabric

Making the Blocks

1. Using a fine-point, black permanent marker and the pattern on page 53 or a blank CD or DVD, center and mark a circle on the nonadhesive side of each interfacing square.

   Note: It may be necessary to use a contrasting bright-colored permanent marker to mark the interfacing used for the brown circles.

2. Place the adhesive side of each interfacing square on the right side of a 5½" fabric square. The marked side will be faceup. Sew on the marked line, overlapping the stitches at the beginning and end. Trim ⅛" from the stitching.

3. Cut a 2½"-long slit in the center of the interfacing, being careful not to cut the fabric. Turn the circle right side out. Carefully run your thumb or finger along the inside seam line to push out the edges. Finger-press the outside edges to create a sharp edge. Do not iron the seam or you will melt the adhesive. It is not necessary to close the opening in the interfacing. Repeat for the remaining circles.

Make 108.

4. Position a circle in one corner of a red square, ⅜" from the edges. Follow the interfacing manufacturer's instructions and iron-temperature recommendations to fuse the shape in place. Repeat for the remaining corners.

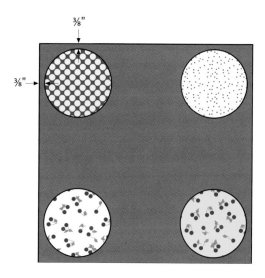

5. Position and press a circle between each of the corner circles on the red square. There should be approximately ⅛" of space between the shapes. Position and press the remaining circle in the center of the red square.

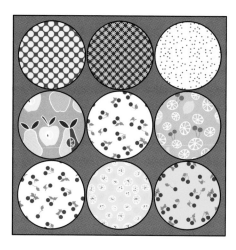

6. Repeat steps 4 and 5 to make a total of 12 blocks. Appliqué the edges of each circle with a narrow buttonhole stitch and coordinating thread. Using a sharp pair of scissors, carefully cut away the red backing and interfacing behind each circle, ¼" from the stitching.

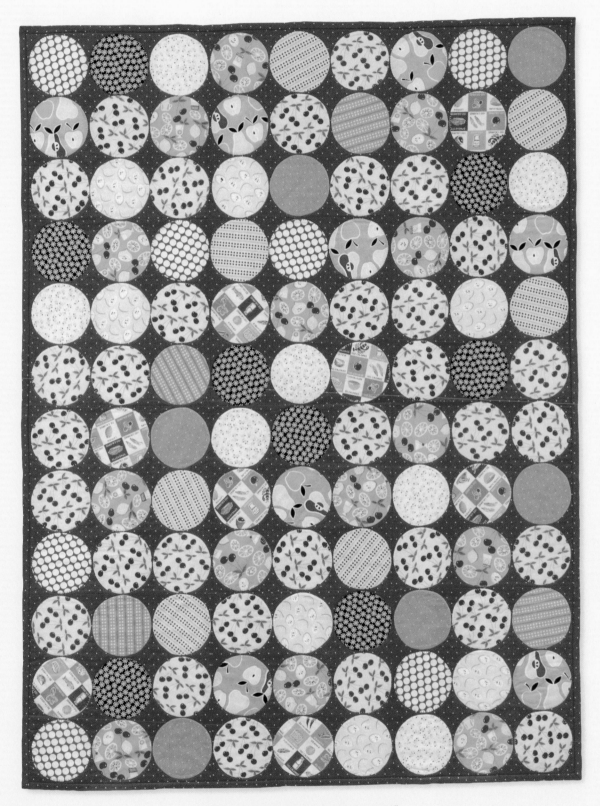

Finished Quilt Size: 44¾" x 59½"

Finished Block Size: 14¾" x 14¾"

Assembling the Quilt Top

Arrange the blocks into four rows of three blocks each. Join the blocks in each row. Press the seam allowances in opposite directions from row to row. Join the rows. Press the seam allowances in one direction.

Finishing

Refer to "Quiltmaking Basics" on page 5 for detailed instructions on finishing techniques, if needed.

1. Piece the quilt backing so that it is 4" to 6" larger than your quilt top.

2. Layer the quilt top with batting and backing, and baste the layers together.

3. Quilt as desired and use the red strips to bind using your favorite method.

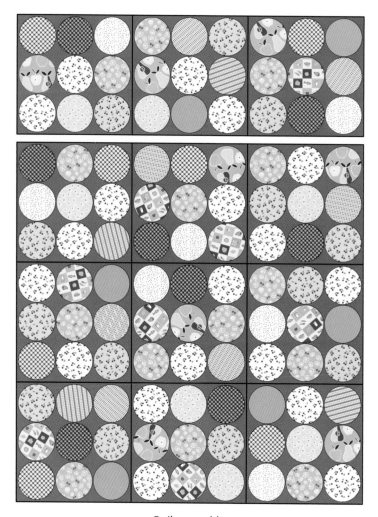

Quilt assembly

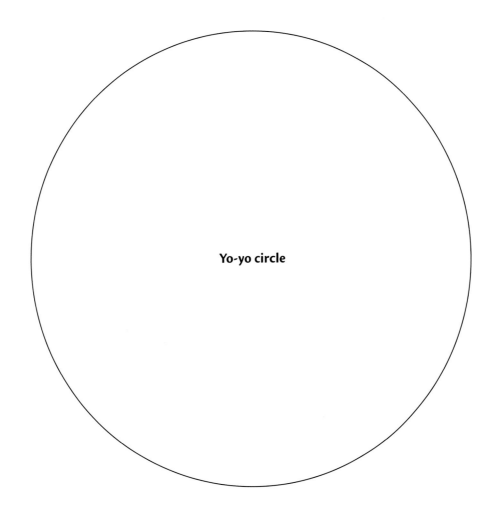

Yo-yo circle

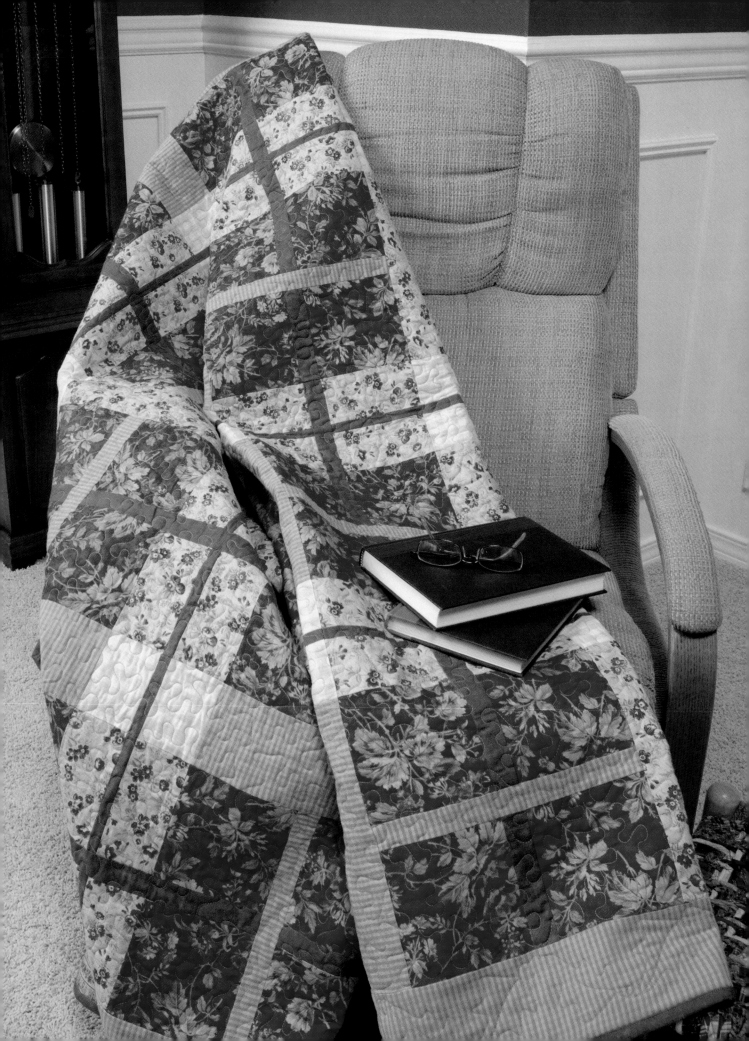

Friendship Plaid

Everything's more fun with a friend, even reading a book. I belong to a great book club. We meet once a month to chat, laugh, and share our mutual addiction to fiction. We read a wide variety of genres, and not everyone has the same literary tastes, but that's what makes it so interesting and fun. Last year we read *Gone with the Wind,* which is enormous, but most of us couldn't put it down. Afterward, we met at my house for a short book discussion; then we lounged in front of the TV to watch the DVD. We thought we were prepared with popcorn and brownies, but it's a long movie, so we ended up ordering pizza as well. So much fun! And I love the fact that it was all about a book.

Teri

Materials

Yardage is based on 42"-wide fabric.

2⅜ yards of red fabric for blocks

2⅛ yards of pink fabric for blocks

2 yards of light green fabric for blocks, sashing, and border

1½ yards of dark green fabric for blocks, sashing, and binding

⅜ yard of beige-and-green check fabric for sashing

5¾ yards of fabric for backing

72" x 95" piece of batting

Cutting

From the red fabric, cut:

14 strips, 5½" x width of fabric; crosscut into:

    96 squares, 5½" x 5½"

From the dark green fabric, cut:

7 strips, 1" x width of fabric; crosscut into:

    15 rectangles, 1" x 4"

    36 rectangles, 1" x 5½"

10 strips, 1½" x width of fabric; crosscut into:

    48 rectangles, 1½" x 5½"

    18 rectangles, 1½" x 6"

9 binding strips, 2½" x width of fabric

From the light green fabric, cut:

4 strips, 4" x width of fabric; crosscut into 12 rectangles, 4" x 11½"

8 strips, 1½" x width of fabric; crosscut into 24 rectangles, 1½" x 11½"

8 strips, 4" x width of fabric

From the pink fabric, cut:

3 strips, 11½" x width of fabric; crosscut into 8 rectangles, 4" x 11½"

6 strips, 5½" x width of fabric; crosscut into 72 rectangles, 3" x 5½"

From the beige-and-green check fabric, cut:

3 strips, 3" x width of fabric; crosscut into 30 rectangles, 3" x 4"

Making the Blocks

It's easier to press your seam allowances if you press after sewing each seam, as explained in these instructions. Do not wait until the entire block is finished before pressing your seam allowances, or it will be difficult to get your iron into the small spaces.

1. Sew together a red 5½" square and a dark green 1½" x 5½" rectangle. Repeat to make a total of 48 units. Press the seam allowances toward the red. Sew another red 5½" square to the opposite side of the green rectangle on all 48 units. Press the seam allowances toward the red.

 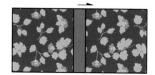

Make 48.

2. Sew together one of the red-and-green units from step 1 and a light green 1½" x 11½" rectangle. Repeat to make a total of 24 units. Press the seam allowances toward the light green. Sew another red unit to the opposite side of the light green rectangle on all 24 units to complete the block. Press the seam allowances toward the light green.

Red block.
Make 24.

3. Sew together a pink 3" x 5½" rectangle and a dark green 1" x 5½" rectangle. Repeat to make a total of 36 units. Press the seam allowances toward the pink. Sew another pink 3" x 5½" rectangle to the opposite side of the dark green strip on all 36 units. Press the seam allowances toward the pink.

Make 36.

4. Sew together one of the pink-and-dark green units from step 3 and one dark green 1½" x 6" rectangle. Repeat to make a total of 18 units. Press the seam allowances toward the dark green. Sew another pink segment to the opposite side of the green rectangle on all 18 units to complete the block. Press the seam allowances toward the dark green.

 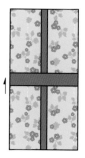

Pink block.
Make 18.

5. Sew together a beige-and-green check 3" x 4" rectangle and a dark green 1" x 4" rectangle. Repeat to make a total of 15 units. Press the seam allowances toward the dark green. Sew a beige-and-green check 3" x 4" rectangle to the opposite side of the green rectangle on all 15 units to complete the block. Press the seam allowances toward the dark green.

Beige block.
Make 15.

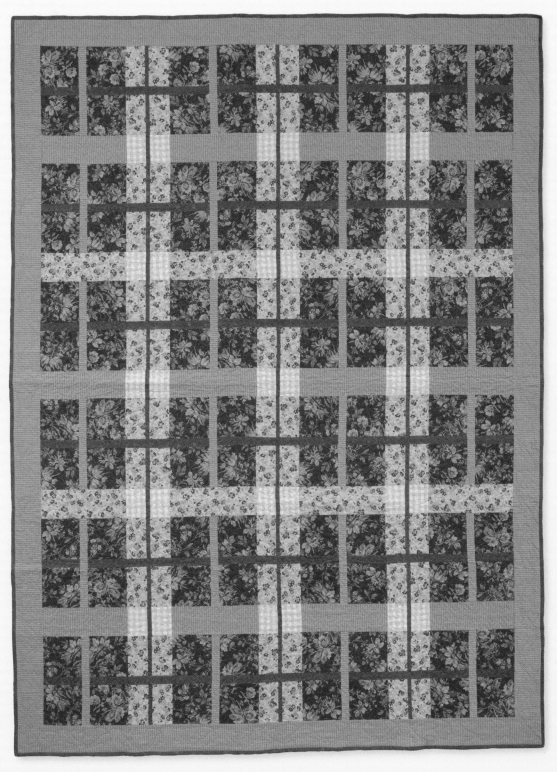

Finished Quilt Size: 68" x 91"

Finished Red Block Size: 11" x 11" • **Finished Pink Block Size:** 5½" x 11"

Finished Beige Block Size: 3½" x 5½"

Assembling the Quilt Top

1. Alternately sew together four red blocks and three pink blocks. Make sure the red blocks are rotated so that the light green stripe is vertical and the dark green stripe is horizontal. Repeat to make a total of six block rows. Press the seam allowances toward the pink blocks.

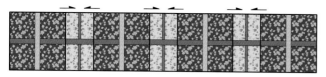

Make 6.

2. Alternately sew together three beige-and-green check blocks and four light green 4" x 11½" rectangles. Repeat to make a total of three green sashing rows. Press the seam allowances toward the light green.

Make 3.

3. Alternately sew together three beige-and-green check blocks and four pink 4" x 11½" rectangles. Repeat to make a total of two pink sashing rows. Press the seam allowances toward the pink.

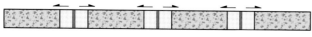

Make 2.

4. Sew the block rows and sashing rows together as shown.

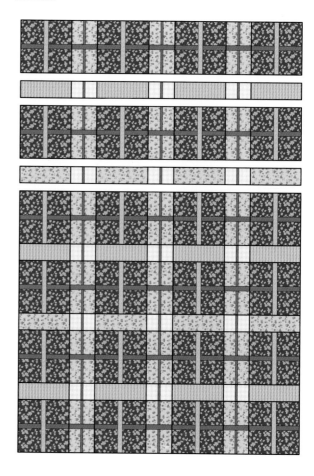

5. Sew the light green 4"-wide strips together end to end to make one long piece. From this piece, cut two border strips, 84" long, and two border strips, 68" long. Sew the 84"-long strips to the sides of the quilt, and then sew the 68"-long strips to the top and bottom of the quilt.

Finishing

Refer to "Quiltmaking Basics" on page 5 for detailed instructions on finishing techniques, if needed.

1. Piece the quilt backing so that it is 4" to 6" larger than your quilt top.

2. Layer the quilt top with batting and backing, and baste the layers together.

3. Quilt as desired and use the dark green strips to bind using your favorite method.

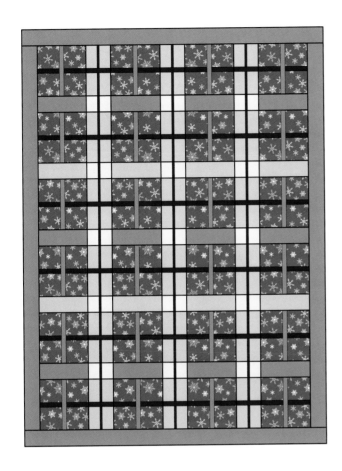

The simple lines of this quilt allow you to easily change the color combination to fit into any decorating scheme. Here are a couple of variations to get you started.

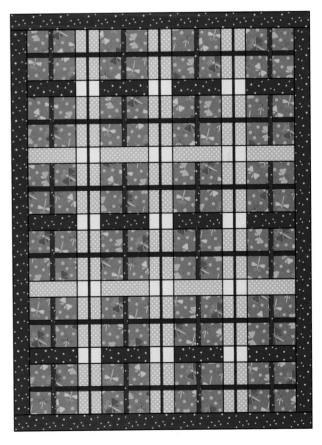

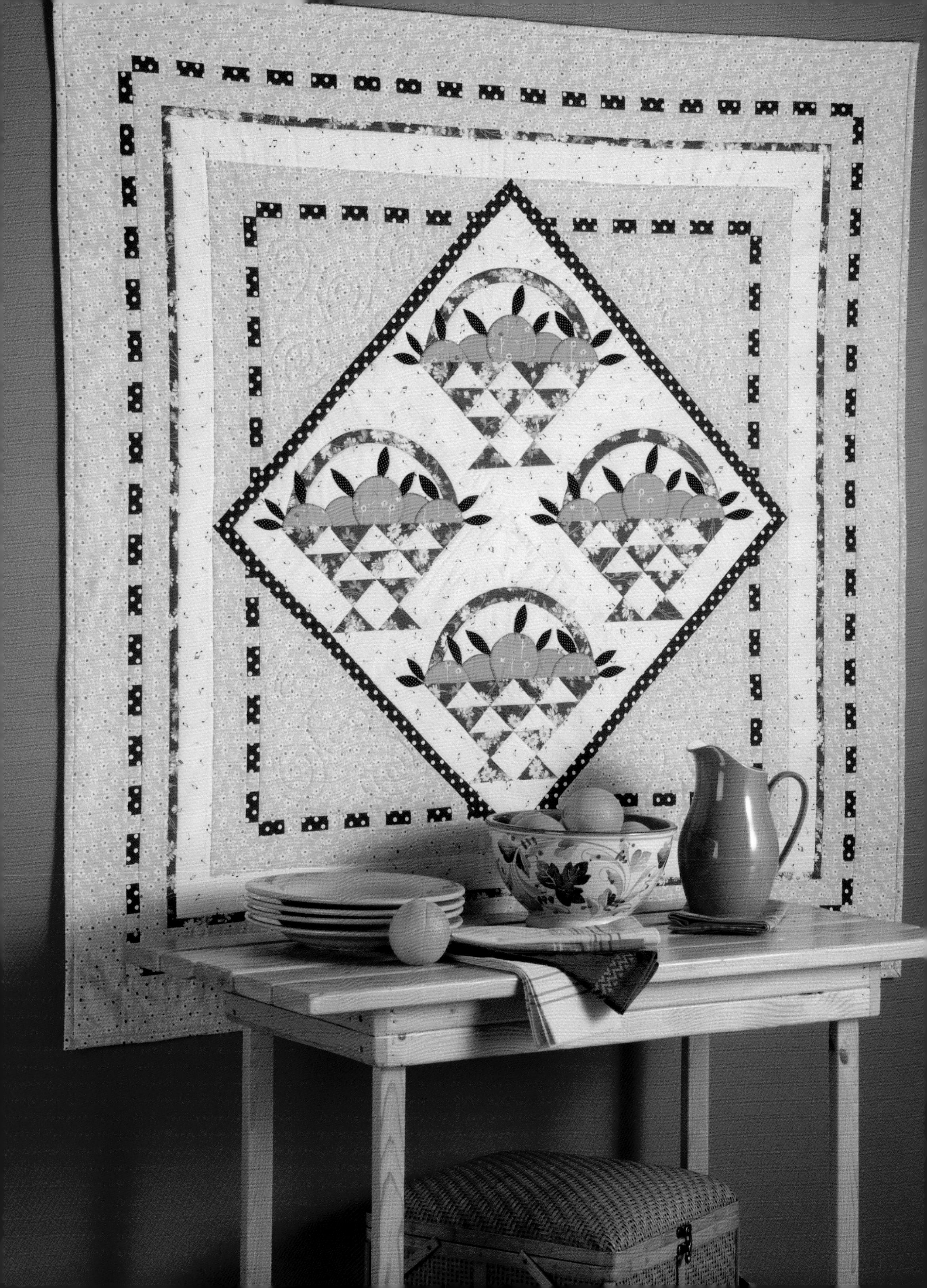

Clementine

Teri and I grew up in Southern California where the growing season extends all year long. Our community was surrounded by strawberry fields and beautiful orange orchards. Dozens of fruit trees of every variety grew on our property, along with a wonderful garden. My favorites were the peaches, nectarines, and strawberries. The milkman delivered our milk on the porch in little old-fashioned bottles, because our mom wanted us to have unpasteurized whole milk. When you pulled the stopper off of the bottle, there was a layer of heavy cream on the top. Every morning I'd pick a few strawberries or a nectarine, slice the fruit, and top it with that cream and a little sugar. You just can't buy a processed, boxed breakfast that will surpass that yummy treat. I think we had at least six orange trees on our property and at least two of every other variety of fruit.

To this day, I just go wild over any pattern that has fruit as the motif. I got excited about this fruit-themed quilt block because the color orange is very popular right now, yet it can be an overpowering color if used in large amounts. The oranges in the baskets have just the right amount of orange.

Barbara

Materials

Yardage is based on 42"-wide fabric.

2½ yards of yellow fabric for quilt center corners, borders, and binding

1⅓ yards of white fabric for blocks and border

⅝ yard of brown fabric for borders

¾ yard of blue fabric for blocks and border

Large scraps *or* 1 fat eighth of brown fabric and 1 fat eighth *each* of 2 different orange fabrics for appliqués

3½ yards of fabric for backing

58" x 58" piece of batting

1⅓ yards of fusible web

Cutting

From the white fabric, cut:

10 squares, 2⅞" x 2⅞"

4 squares, 2½" x 2½"

8 rectangles, 2½" x 8⅞"

2 squares, 4⅞" x 4⅞"; cut once diagonally to yield 4 triangles

2 squares, 12⅞" x 12⅞"; cut once diagonally to yield 4 triangles

2 strips, 2½" x 36½"

2 strips, 2½" x 40½"

From the blue fabric, cut:*

22 squares, 2⅞" x 2⅞"; cut *12* squares in half diagonally to yield 24 triangles

2 strips, 1" x 40½"

2 strips, 1" x 41½"

*The remaining blue fabric will be used for basket-handle appliqués.

- 61 -

From the brown fabric, cut:

2 strips, 1¼" x 24½"

2 strips, 1¼" x 26"

6 strips, 2" x width of fabric

From the yellow fabric, cut:

6 strips, 1½" x width of fabric

2 squares, 13⅜" x 13⅜"; cut once diagonally to yield
    4 triangles

4 pieces, 2½" x 16⅞"

4 pieces, 2½" x 18⅞"

2 squares, 1¼" x 1¼"

5 strips, 2" x width of fabric

5 strips, 3½" x width of fabric

6 binding strips, 2½" x width of fabric

Making the Blocks

1. Use a pencil and ruler to draw a diagonal line on the wrong side of the 10 white 2⅞" squares. Place each white square with a blue 2⅞" square, right sides together and raw edges even. Sew ¼" away from both sides of the drawn line. Cut on the line. Press the seam allowances open. You will end up with 20 triangle-square units.

Make 20.

2. Sew together five triangle-square units, four blue triangles, and one white 2½" square as shown. Repeat to make a total of four basket units.

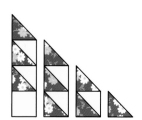 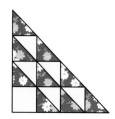

Make 4.

3. Sew the remaining blue triangles to one end of each of the white 2½" x 8⅞" rectangles to make four basket-base units and four reversed basket-base units.

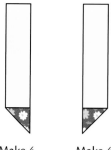

Make 4.   Make 4.

4. With the lower edges aligned, stitch the basket-base units to the sides of each basket unit. Trim the base units even with the top of the baskets.

Trim.

5. Sew a white 4⅞" triangle to the bottom of each basket to complete the bottom half of the block.

6. Refer to "Using Fusible Web" on page 7 and use the patterns on page 67 to prepare the appliqués. From the blue fabric, make four handles. Make eight of orange A from one of the orange fabrics. Make eight of orange B and four of orange C from the other orange fabric. From the brown fabric, make 20 small leaves and 16 large leaves.

Finished Quilt Size: 52" x 52"

Finished Block Size: 12" x 12"

7. Refer to the placement guide on page 67 to apply the appliqué pieces to each white 12⅞" triangle as follows to make the top half of the blocks:

   a. Center a handle along the long edge of the triangle. Iron to fuse in place. Appliqué the edges with a buttonhole stitch and blue thread.

   b. Position the oranges on the triangle, overlapping the shapes and aligning the orange straight edges with the triangle straight edge. Iron to fuse in place.

   c. Add seven of the leaves to the triangle; the remaining two end leaves will be applied after the block halves are sewn together. Iron to fuse in place.

   d. Appliqué the edges of the oranges and leaves with a buttonhole stitch and brown thread.

8. Sew each top half to a basket bottom half.

9. Position, fuse, and appliqué the two remaining small leaves to each block, overlapping the seam allowance.

Assembling the Quilt Top

1. Sew the blocks together in two rows of two blocks each. Press the seam allowances in opposite directions.

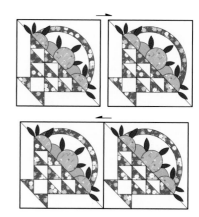

2. Sew the brown 1¼" x 24½" strips to the opposite sides of the quilt center, and then sew the brown 1¼" x 26" strips to the remaining opposite sides of the quilt center.

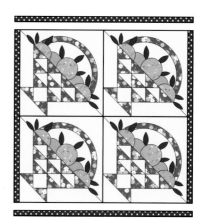

3. Alternately sew the brown 2"-wide strips and yellow 1½"-wide strips together to make a strip set. Press the seam allowances open. Crosscut the strip set into 20 border segments, 1¼" wide.

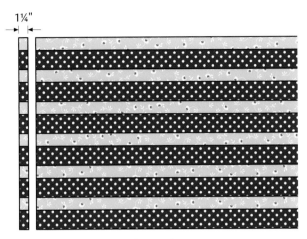

1¼"

Make 1 strip set.
Cut 20 segments.

4. Position a yellow 13⅜" triangle as shown so that the short sides are on the bottom and left. Sew a border segment to the bottom of the triangle, aligning the brown end of the segment with the corner of the triangle. The segment will extend beyond the end of the triangle but will be trimmed later. Trim ¼" off of the yellow end of another pieced border segment. Stitch the border to the left side of the yellow triangle, aligning the trimmed yellow end with the corner. Again, the strip will be longer than the triangle but will be trimmed later.

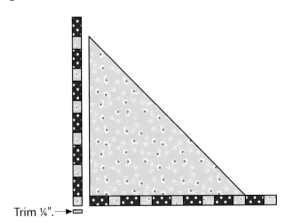

Trim ¼".

5. Sew a yellow 2½" x 16⅞" piece to the bottom of the triangle. It also will be longer than the triangle. Sew a yellow 2½" x 18⅞" piece to the left side of the triangle. Trim the borders even with the long edge of the triangle.

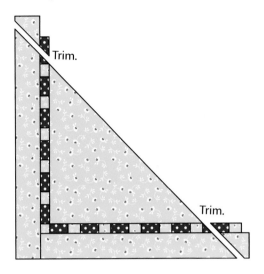

Trim.

Trim.

6. Repeat steps 4 and 5 to make a total of four quilt center corners.

7. Sew two corners to opposite sides of the quilt center. Repeat for the remaining corners.

8. Refer to the assembly diagram below to sew the white 2½" x 36½" border strips to the sides of the quilt, and then sew the white 2½" x 40½" border strips to the top and bottom of the quilt. Sew the blue 1" x 40½" border strips to the sides of the quilt, and then sew the blue 1" x 41½" border strips to the top and bottom of the quilt.

9. Sew the yellow 2"-wide strips together end to end to make one long piece. From this piece, cut two border strips, 41½" long, and two border strips, 44½" long. Sew the 41½"-long strips to the sides of the quilt, and then sew the 44½"-long strips to the top and bottom of the quilt.

10. Sew three strip-pieced segments together end to end so that the colors alternate. Repeat to make a total of four border strips.

Make 4.

11. Remove the yellow rectangle from the end of two pieced border strips. Sew these border strips to the sides of the quilt. Sew a yellow 1¼" square to the brown end of the remaining two pieced border strips. Trim ¼" off the yellow rectangle at the opposite end of each pieced border. Stitch the pieced borders to the top and bottom of the quilt.

12. Sew the yellow 3½"-wide strips together end to end to make one long piece. From this piece, cut two border strips, 3½" x 46", and two border strips, 3½" x 52". Sew the 46"-long strips to the sides of the quilt, and then sew the 52"-long strips to the top and bottom of the quilt.

Finishing

Refer to "Quiltmaking Basics" on page 5 for detailed instructions on finishing techniques, if needed.

1. Piece the quilt backing so that it is 4" to 6" larger than your quilt top.

2. Layer the quilt top with batting and backing, and baste the layers together.

3. Quilt as desired and use the yellow strips to bind using your favorite method.

Quilt assembly

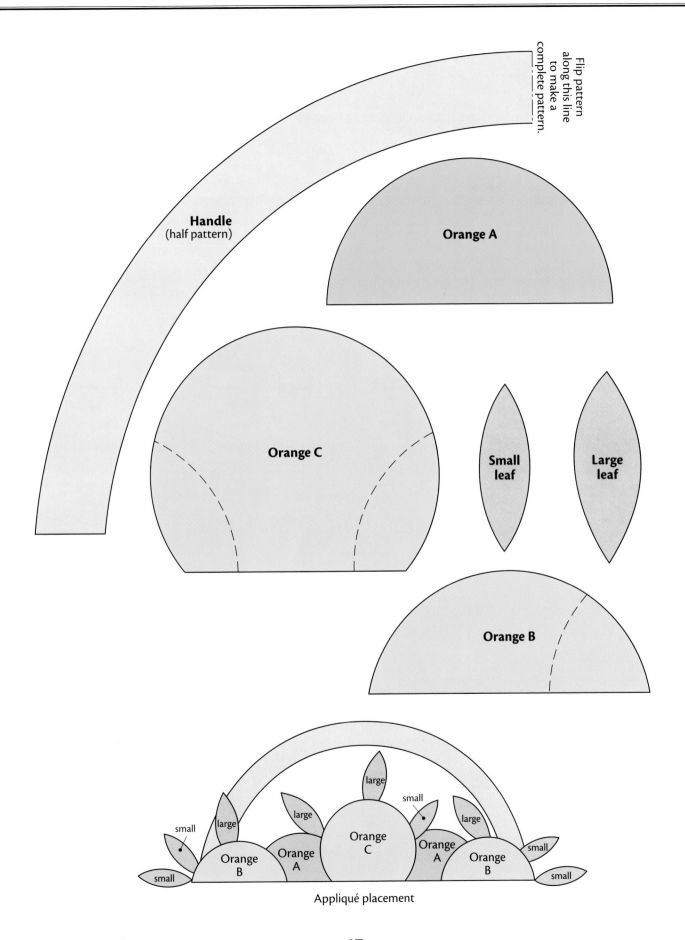

Flip pattern along this line to make a complete pattern.

Handle
(half pattern)

Orange A

Orange C

Small leaf

Large leaf

Orange B

large

small

large

large

small

large

small

small

Orange B

Orange A

Orange C

Orange A

Orange B

small

small

Appliqué placement

I'm fortunate to live near the ocean in Southern California. The beach is such an incredibly relaxing place. I take the kids once a week in the summer, usually meeting up with friends. The moms relax in beach chairs while the kids play in the sand and surf. Sometimes I feel stressed as we leave the house, making sure we have everything, but the minute my feet hit the sand, the tension slides right off me. Our favorite summer day is the Fourth of July, when we join a large group of friends for a full day of sun, surf, hot dogs, and fireworks. It's insanely crowded, of course, so we have to go early to stake our claim. I spread out beach blankets in a clear statement of sand ownership. I made this beach blanket to be fast, fun, and colorful. Quilting doesn't get any easier than this. Enjoy summer!

Teri

Materials

Yardage is based on 42"-wide fabric.

2¼ yards of ivory fabric for blocks

2 yards of red fabric for blocks and binding

1½ yards of blue fabric for blocks

1⅛ yards of green fabric for blocks

4¾ yards of fabric for backing

76" x 76" piece of batting

Cutting

From the ivory fabric, cut:

48 strips, 1½" x width of fabric

From the green fabric, cut:

24 strips, 1½" x width of fabric

From the red fabric, cut:

18 strips, 2½" x width of fabric; crosscut into
54 rectangles, 2½" x 12½"

8 binding strips, 2½" x width of fabric

From the blue fabric, cut:

18 strips, 2½" x width of fabric; crosscut into
54 rectangles, 2½" x 12½"

Making the Blocks

1. Sew together two ivory strips and one green strip along the long edges to make a strip set. Repeat to make a total of 24 strip sets. Crosscut the strip sets into 72 segments, 12½" long.

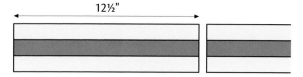

12½"

Make 24 strip sets.
Cut 72 segments.

2. Sew together two of the strip-set segments and three red 2½" x 12½" rectangles. Repeat to make a total of 18 blocks.

Make 18.

3. Sew together two of the strip-set segments and three blue 2½" x 12½" rectangles. Repeat to make a total of 18 blocks.

Make 18.

Assembling the Quilt Top

1. Alternately sew together three red blocks and three blue blocks, rotating the red blocks so the stripes are horizontal. Repeat to make a total of six rows.

Make 6.

2. Sew the rows together, reversing every other row so the red and blue blocks alternate from row to row.

Finishing

Refer to "Quiltmaking Basics" on page 5 for detailed instructions on finishing techniques, if needed.

1. Piece the quilt backing so that it is 4" to 6" larger than your quilt top.

2. Layer the quilt top with batting and backing, and baste the layers together.

3. Quilt as desired and use the red strips to bind using your favorite method.

Finished Quilt Size: 72½" x 72½"

Finished Block Size: 12" x 12"

The other night my sister Carol called me over to help her peel a batch of apples to make some homemade jam. I brought along my automated apple-peeling gizmo. It was 10 o'clock at night, and what a fiasco it was. The apples kept mushing up and making a terrible mess. We finally figured out that half of the batch was actually little round green pears. We laughed so hard. We were two intelligent gals, trying to cook way too late in the evening without a clue of what we were doing. I went home that night and sketched out my "wild pears" in honor of our wild pear night. I like that about designing. You can get a wild idea anywhere!

Barbara

Materials

Yardage is based on 42"-wide fabric.

1⅔ yards of blue fabric for blocks and outer border

1¾ yards of off-white fabric for block backgrounds and pieced border

1⅛ yards of brown fabric for stems, pieced border, and binding

1 yard of cream fabric for sashing and inner border

½ yard of yellow fabric for pears

⅛ yard *each* of two green fabrics for leaves

3⅞ yards of fabric for backing

66" x 66" piece of batting

1⅞ yards of fusible web

Cutting

From the blue fabric, cut:

32 rectangles, 2" x 8"

32 rectangles, 2" x 11"

6 strips, 3" x width of fabric

From the off-white fabric, cut:

16 squares, 8" x 8"

10 strips, 2" x width of fabric

8 squares, 2" x 2"

From the cream fabric, cut:

12 rectangles, 2¼" x 11"

10 strips, 2¼" x width of fabric

From the brown fabric, cut:*

5 strips, 2" x width of fabric

7 binding strips, 2½" x width of fabric

*The remaining brown fabric will be used for stem appliqués.

Making the Blocks

1. Sew a blue 2" x 8" rectangle to the sides of an off-white 8" square. Press the seam allowances toward the blue. Sew the blue 2" x 11" rectangles to the top and bottom of the square. Press the seam allowances toward the blue. Repeat to make a total of 16 background squares.

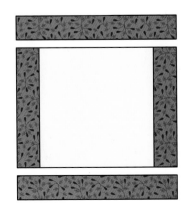

2. Refer to "Using Fusible Web" on page 7 and use the patterns on page 77 to prepare the appliqués. Make 16 pears from the yellow fabric, 16 stems from the remaining brown fabric, 16 of leaf A from one green fabric, and 16 of leaf B from the other green fabric.

3. Refer to the placement guide to position the shapes on the background squares. Iron to fuse in place. Appliqué the edges of each shape using a narrow buttonhole stitch and brown thread.

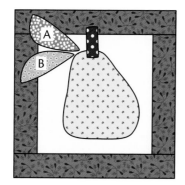

Appliqué placement

Assembling the Quilt Top

1. Alternately join four blocks and three cream 2¼" x 11" rectangles. Repeat to make a total of four block rows.

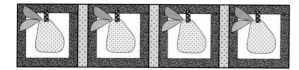

Make 4.

2. Sew the cream 2¼"-wide strips together end to end to make one long piece. From this piece, cut five sashing/border strips, 47¾" long, and two border strips, 51¼" long. Alternately join the block rows and 47¾"-long sashing strips.

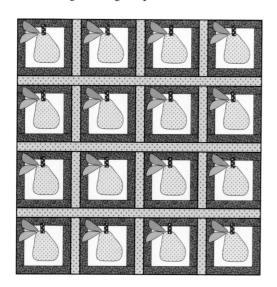

3. Sew the remaining 47¾"-long strips to the sides of the quilt, and then sew the 51¼"-long strips to the top and bottom of the quilt.

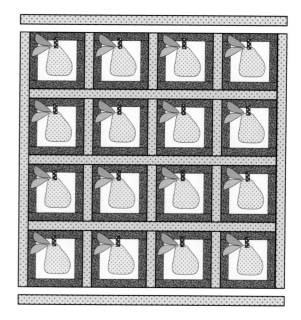

4. Sew one brown and two off-white 2"-wide strips together along the long edges to make a strip set. Repeat to make a total of five strip sets. Crosscut the strip sets into 100 segments, 2" wide.

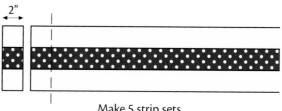

Make 5 strip sets.
Cut 100 segments.

5. Join 24 segments together as shown. Repeat to make a total of two pieced strips for the side borders. Sew an additional off-white 2" square to each end of the strips. Join 26 units in the same manner. Repeat to make a total of two pieced strips for the top and bottom borders. Sew an additional off-white 2" square to each end of the strips. Press the seam allowances of each strip open. Press gently to avoid stretching the bias edges.

Finished Quilt Size: 60" x 60"

Finished Block Size: 10½" x 10½"

6. Trim the top, bottom, and ends of each pieced border ¼" outside the points of the brown squares. The long edges are on the bias and will stretch easily. Handle them with care to keep the borders the proper size.

7. Sew the side pieced borders to the sides of the quilt, and then sew the top and bottom pieced borders to the top and bottom of the quilt. **Hint:** Sew with the pieced border on the bottom to keep it from stretching out of shape.

8. Sew the blue 3"-wide strips together end to end to make one long piece. From this piece, cut two border strips, 55½" long, and two border strips, 60½" long. Sew the 55½"-long strips to the sides of the quilt, and then sew the 60½"-long strips to the top and bottom of the quilt.

Finishing

Refer to "Quiltmaking Basics" on page 5 for detailed instructions on finishing techniques, if needed.

1. Piece the quilt backing so that it is 4" to 6" larger than your quilt top.

2. Layer the quilt top with batting and backing, and baste the layers together.

3. Quilt as desired and use the brown strips to bind using your favorite method.

Quilt assembly

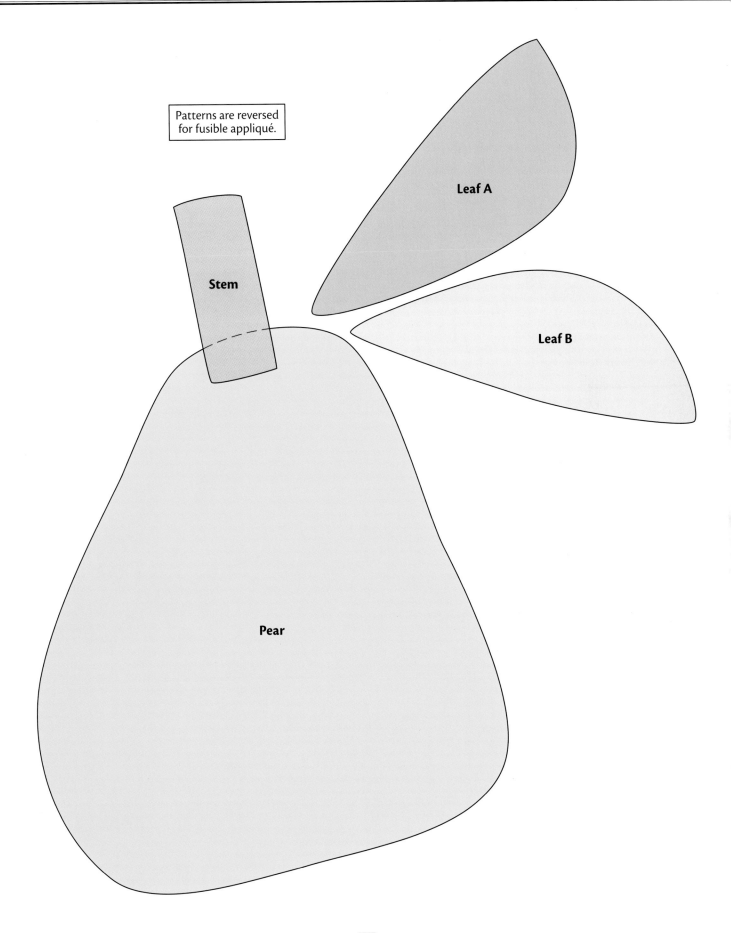

Patterns are reversed
for fusible appliqué.

Leaf A

Stem

Leaf B

Pear

Spring Awakening

I love spring. The garden yawns and stretches for a few weeks, and then everything seems to wake up and smile. I have 30 rosebushes and wait eagerly every year for the first pink and white petals to appear. Last year I went out of town just as the buds were opening, and when I returned a week later, my garden was overflowing with glorious roses. The earth just feels happier in the spring, and the mood is infectious. We all feel it. It's the perfect time to sew a new quilt out of fresh, pretty fabrics. This one is simple yet filled with springtime charm. Just looking at it fills me with joy.

Teri

Materials

Yardage is based on 42"-wide fabric. This quilt is scrappy, but I kept the color selection very limited so the overall pattern of the quilt wouldn't get lost in the chaos. For example, there are four different brown fabrics in the quilt, but they are all very similar shades. The ivory fabric is not scrappy; I used the same ivory fabric in all the patchwork blocks.

2⅝ yards of ivory print for blocks

2⅛ yards of floral for inner border

1¼ yards of red print for outer border and binding

¼ yard *each* of 4 different-but-similar brown fabrics

¼ yard *each* of 4 different-but-similar green fabrics

¼ yard *each* of 4 different-but-similar pink fabrics

¼ yard *each* of 4 different-but-similar red fabrics

8 yards of fabric for backing

86" x 86" piece of batting

Cutting

From the ivory print, cut:

8 strips, 4⅞" x width of fabric; crosscut into 64 squares, 4⅞" x 4⅞"

18 strips, 2½" x width of fabric; crosscut into 256 squares, 2½" x 2½"

From the 4 different-but-similar brown fabrics, cut a *total* of 16 sets, with each set cut from the same fabric and consisting of:

1 square, 4⅞" x 4⅞"

4 squares, 2½" x 2½"

From the 4 different-but-similar green fabrics, cut a *total* of 16 sets, with each set cut from the same fabric and consisting of:

1 square, 4⅞" x 4⅞"

4 squares, 2½" x 2½"

From the 4 different-but-similar pink fabrics, cut a *total* of 16 sets, with each set cut from the same fabric and consisting of:

1 square, 4⅞" x 4⅞"

4 squares, 2½" x 2½"

From the 4 different-but-similar red fabrics, cut a *total* of 16 sets, with each set cut from the same fabric and consisting of:

1 square, 4⅞" x 4⅞"

4 squares, 2½" x 2½"

From the floral, cut:

8 strips, 8½" x width of fabric

From the red print, cut:

9 strips, 1½" x width of fabric

9 binding strips, 2½" x width of fabric

Making the Blocks

1. Use a pencil and ruler to draw a diagonal line on the wrong side of the ivory 4⅞" squares.

2. Using the pieces from one brown set, place an ivory 4⅞" square with the brown 4⅞" square, right sides together and raw edges even. Sew ¼" away from both sides of the drawn line. Cut on the line. Press the seam allowances toward the brown fabric. You will end up with two triangle-square units.

Make 2.

3. Sew each brown 2½" square in the set to an ivory 2½" square to make a two-patch unit. Press the seam allowances toward the brown fabric.

Make 4.

4. Sew together two two-patch units as shown to create a four-patch unit. Repeat to make a total of two units. Press the seam allowances in either direction.

Make 2.

5. Sew each triangle-square unit to a four-patch unit. Press the seam allowances toward the four-patch unit.

Make 2.

6. Sew the step 5 units together as shown to complete the block. Press the seam allowance in either direction.

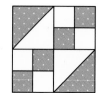

7. Repeat steps 2–6 with the remaining brown, green, pink, and red sets to make a total of 64 blocks.

Assembling the Quilt Top

1. Arrange the blocks on the floor or a design wall in quadrants as shown. Pay close attention to the way the blocks are rotated so they create the overall quilt design. To remember block placement, write the numbers 1–64 on the blocks with a water-soluble fabric marker, or pin paper labels onto the blocks.

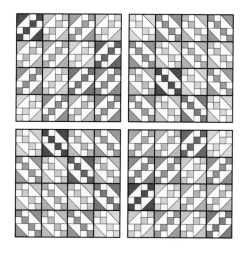

2. Sew together the blocks in each quadrant; then sew the quadrants together to complete the quilt center.

3. Sew the floral 8½"-wide strips together end to end to create one long piece. From this piece, cut two border strips, 64½" long, and two border strips, 80½" long. Sew the 64½"-long strips to the sides of the quilt. Sew the 80½"-long strips to the top and bottom of the quilt.

4. Join the red 1½"-wide strips together end to end to create one long piece. From this piece, cut two border strips, 80½" long, and two border strips, 82½" long. Sew the 80½"-long strips to the sides of the quilt. Sew the 82½"-long strips to the top and bottom of the quilt.

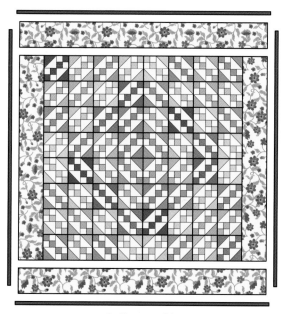

Quilt assembly

Finished Quilt Size: 82½" x 82½"

Finished Block Size: 8" x 8"

Finishing

Refer to "Quiltmaking Basics" on page 5 for detailed instructions on finishing techniques, if needed.

1. Piece the quilt backing so that it is 4" to 6" larger than your quilt top.

2. Layer the quilt top with batting and backing, and baste the layers together.

3. Quilt as desired and use the red strips to bind using your favorite method.

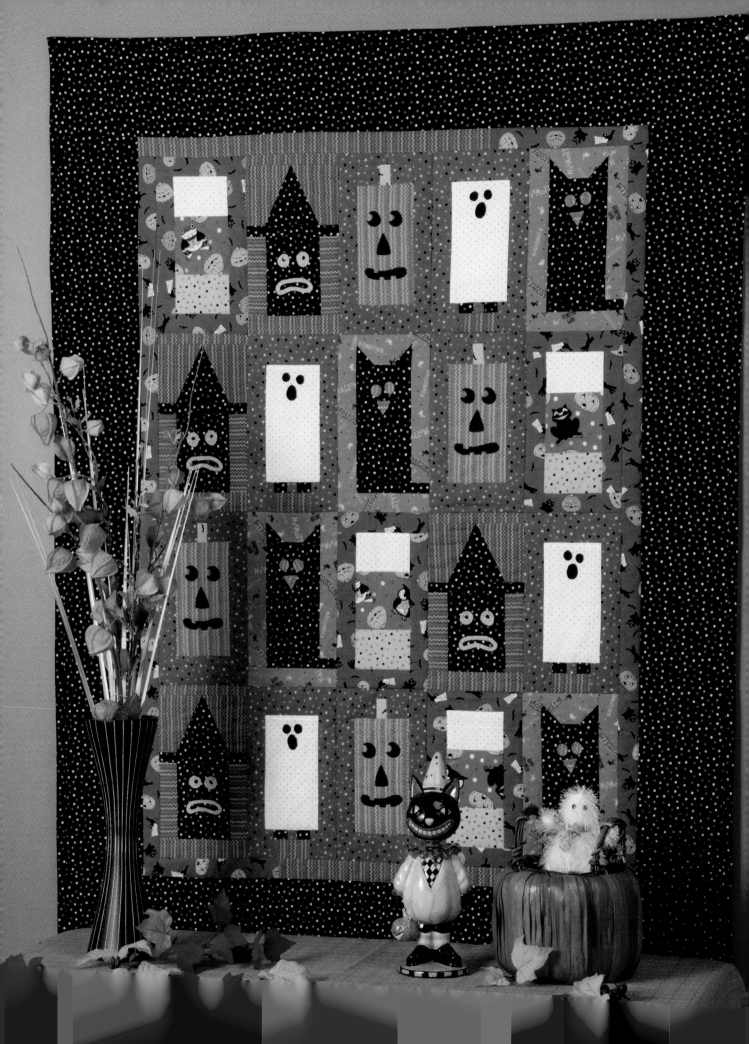

Teri and I used to have a blast at the annual fall trade show in Houston, Texas. We had many giggly late nights with our quilting girlfriends and made many wonderful memories. The only sad thing was that the event was always scheduled over Halloween. This year, my college-aged daughter gave me a bad time for not being around during Halloween over the years. She chewed me out quite firmly and informed me, "You *will* decorate the house with lots of holiday cheer for my future children."

I just heard that my new grandson will be dressed as a proud banana for Halloween this year, so I'd better get busy stringing those webs and spiders! It's exciting to know that my job is to pass on our wonderful holiday traditions and to create warm memories for the next generation. Holiday quilts are one of my favorite projects to design, and the job is easy when you find cute fabrics.

Barbara

Materials

Yardage is based on 42"-wide fabric.

1⅝ yards of black fabric for blocks, outer border, and binding

6 fat quarters of assorted green fabrics for block backgrounds and inner border

1 fat quarter of white fabric for ghosts and candy corn

Large scraps of two orange fabrics for pumpkins, candy corn, and cat facial details

Scraps of two yellow fabrics for candy corn and pumpkin stems

Scrap of light green for witch facial details

Scrap of black solid fabric for pumpkin and ghost facial details

1⅝ yards of fabric for backing

41" x 52" piece of batting

⅜ yard of fusible web

Cutting

Hint: Store the pieces for each block in a plastic bag labeled with the block name. Patterns for the witch hat and witch hat background are on page 89.

From the green fat quarter for the Candy Corn block backgrounds, cut:

8 rectangles, 1½" x 7½"

8 rectangles, 1½" x 5½"

From the green fat quarter for the Pumpkin block backgrounds, cut:

8 rectangles, 1½" x 8"

8 rectangles, 1½" x 1¾"

4 rectangles, 2" x 5½"

4 rectangles, 1" x 3½"

From the green fat quarter for the Ghost block backgrounds, cut:

4 rectangles, 2" x 5½"

8 squares, 2" x 2"

8 rectangles, 1½" x 6½"

4 rectangles, 1½" x 2½"

4 squares, 1" x 1"

From the green fat quarter for the Cat block backgrounds, cut:

4 rectangles, 2" x 3½"

4 rectangles, 1½" x 8½"

4 rectangles, 1½" x 8"

4 rectangles, 1½" x 5½"

From the green fat quarter for the Witch block backgrounds, cut:

4 hat background template pieces

4 hat background reversed template pieces

4 rectangles, 1½" x 5½"

8 rectangles, 1½" x 4½"

4 rectangles, 1" x 5½"

From the remainder of the assorted green fat quarters, cut a *total* of:

7 strips, 1½" x 20" (inner border)

From the black fabric, cut:

5 binding strips, 2½" x width of fabric

2 strips, 5" x 38½" (outer border)

2 strips, 5" x 36½" (outer border)

4 rectangles, 3½" x 6½" (cat)

8 squares, 1½" x 1½" (cat)

4 rectangles, 1" x 4½" (cat)

4 rectangles, 3½" x 4½" (witch)

4 rectangles, 1" x 5½" (witch)

4 hat template pieces (witch)

8 rectangles, 1" x 1¼" (ghost)

From the white fat quarter, cut:

4 rectangles, 3½" x 6½" (ghosts)

4 rectangles, 2½" x 3½" (candy corn)

From the orange scraps, cut a *total* of:

4 squares, 3½" x 3½" (candy corn)

4 rectangles, 3½" x 6½" (pumpkins)

From the yellow scraps, cut a *total* of:

4 rectangles, 2½" x 3½" (candy corn)

4 rectangles, 1" x 1½" (pumpkin stems)

Making the Blocks

Press all seam allowances open as you add each piece.

Candy Corn Blocks

1. Sew a white 2½" x 3½" rectangle to the top of each orange 3½" square. Join a yellow 2½" x 3½" rectangle to the bottom of each orange square.

2. Sew green 1½" x 7½" rectangles to the sides, and then sew a green 1½" x 5½" rectangle to the top and bottom of the units.

Finished Quilt Size: 36½" x 47½"

Finished Block Size: 5" x 9"

Pumpkin Blocks

1. Sew green 1½" x 1¾" rectangles to the sides of each yellow 1" x 1½" rectangle to make the stem unit. Sew a stem unit to the top of each orange 3½" x 6½" rectangle. Add a green 1" x 3½" rectangle to the top of the stem units.

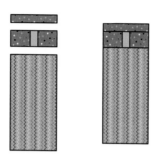

2. Sew green 1½" x 8" rectangles to the sides, and then sew a green 2" x 5½" rectangle to the bottom of the units.

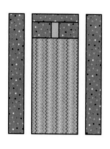 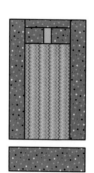

Ghost Blocks

1. Sew black 1" x 1¼" rectangles to the sides of each green 1" square. Sew a green 1½" x 2½" rectangle to the bottom of each unit. Sew green 2" squares to the sides to complete the shoe units.

2. Sew green 1½" x 6½" rectangles to the sides of each white 3½" x 6½" rectangle. To each of these units, join a shoe unit to the bottom and a green 2" x 5½" rectangle to the top.

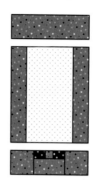 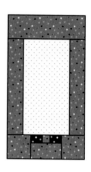

Cat Blocks

1. Place a black 1½" square on the lower-left corner of each green 2" x 3½" rectangle, right sides together. Sew diagonally across the square as shown. Cut off the outer triangle, leaving a ¼" seam allowance. Press the seam allowance open. Repeat on the lower-right corner of each rectangle to complete the ear units.

2. Sew an ear unit to the top of each black 3½" x 6½" rectangle. For each of these units, sew a green 1½" x 8" rectangle to the right side and a black 1" x 4½" rectangle to the bottom.

3. Sew a green 1½" x 8½" rectangle to the left side of each unit. Sew a green 1½" x 5½" rectangle to the bottom of each unit.

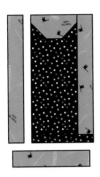 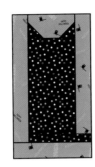

Witch Blocks

1. Sew a green witch background piece and a reversed witch background piece to the sides of each black hat piece.

2. Sew a black 1" x 5½" rectangle to the bottom of the hat. Join a green 1" x 5½" rectangle to the top to complete the hat units.

3. Sew green 1½" x 4½" rectangles to the sides of each black 3½" x 4½" rectangle. Sew a green 1½" x 5½" rectangle to the bottom of each unit. Join the hat units to the top of these units.

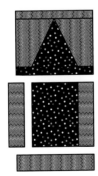 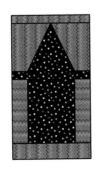

Adding the Appliqués

Refer to "Using Fusible Web" on page 7 and use the patterns on page 89 to prepare the appliqués. From the black scrap, make eight pumpkin eyes, four pumpkin noses, four pumpkin mouths, eight ghost eyes, and four ghost mouths. From the remaining orange fabric for the pumpkins, make eight cat eyes and four cat noses. From the scrap of light green, make eight witch eyes and four witch mouths. Refer to the photo on page 85 to position the shapes on the appropriate blocks. Iron to fuse in place. Appliqué the edges of each piece with a narrow buttonhole stitch and coordinating thread.

Assembling the Quilt Top

1. Sew the blocks into four rows of five blocks each as shown. Sew the rows together.

2. Sew the assorted green 1½" x 20" strips together end to end in random order to make one long piece. From this piece, cut two border strips, 36½" long, and two border strips, 27½" long. Sew the 36½"-long strips to the sides of the quilt, and then sew the 27½"-long strips to the top and bottom of the quilt.

3. Sew the black 5" x 38½" strips to the sides of the quilt, and sew the black 5" x 36½" strips to the top and bottom of the quilt.

Finishing

Refer to "Quiltmaking Basics" on page 5 for detailed instructions on finishing techniques, if needed.

1. Layer the quilt top with batting and backing, and baste the layers together.

2. Quilt as desired and use the black strips to bind using your favorite method.

Quilt assembly

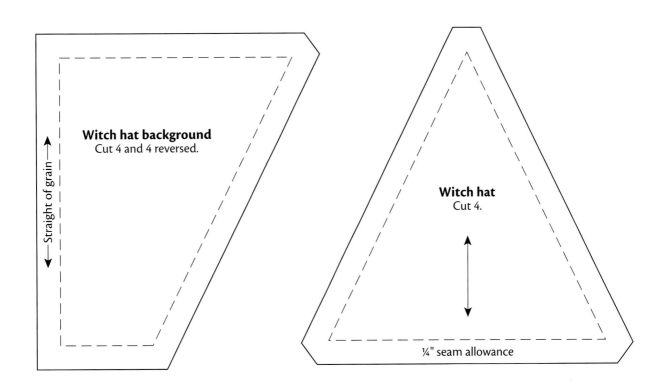

Witch hat background
Cut 4 and 4 reversed.

← Straight of grain →

Witch hat
Cut 4.

¼" seam allowance

Patterns are reversed for fusible appliqué.

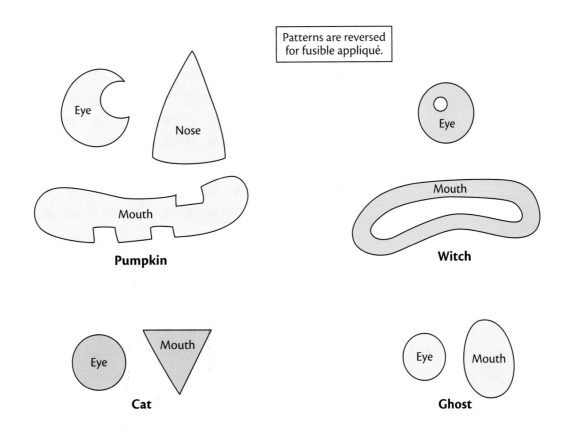

Eye

Nose

Mouth

Pumpkin

Eye

Mouth

Witch

Eye

Mouth

Cat

Eye

Mouth

Ghost

Christmas Festival

There's something magical about the smell of a Christmas tree in the house and the twinkle of tiny lights. One of my most memorable Christmases, as a teenager, was the year my father had health problems and money was very tight. It was late December before anyone thought about buying a tree. We counted our pennies and decided we could afford $20. We set out on the impossible quest and visited many picked-over tree lots without success. Finally, tired and discouraged, we stopped at the local hardware store. A stunning Douglas fir stood in the back corner, tagged with the unbelievable price of $19.99. We laughed and cheered and knew it was our Christmas miracle. There weren't very many presents under the tree that year, but we didn't care. Our gifts were the joy and love we felt in our home.

Teri

Materials

Yardage is based on 42"-wide fabric.

3 yards of ivory fabric for block backgrounds

3 yards of green fabric for trees, border, and binding

2⅔ yards of red fabric for block backgrounds

⅞ yard of pale gold fabric for stars

5¼ yards of fabric for backing

68" x 84" piece of batting

3½ yards of fusible web

Cutting

From the red fabric, cut:

5 strips, 8½" x width of fabric; crosscut into 20 squares, 8½" x 8½"

12 strips, 3½" x width of fabric; crosscut into 124 squares, 3½" x 3½"

From the ivory fabric, cut:

11 strips, 8½" x width of fabric; crosscut into 43 squares, 8½" x 8½"

From the green fabric, cut:*

8 strips, 4½" x width of fabric

8 binding strips, 2½" x width of fabric

*The remaining green fabric will be used for Christmas tree appliqués.

Making the Blocks

1. Refer to "Using Fusible Web" on page 7 and use the patterns on page 94 to prepare the appliqués. Make 20 stars from the pale gold fabric and 31 trees from the remaining green fabric. To reduce bulk, cut out the center of the fusible paper shapes before ironing them to the wrong side of the fabrics.

2. Use a sharp pencil and ruler to draw a line across the diagonal on the wrong side of the red 3½" squares. Position a red square on one corner of an ivory 8½" square, right sides together and raw edges even. Sew on the drawn line. Cut off the outer corner, leaving a ¼" seam allowance. Press the red triangle back. Repeat on all four corners. Repeat

to make a total of 31 blocks. You will have 12 ivory squares remaining.

 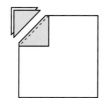

Make 31.

3. Center a tree appliqué on each of the 31 pieced blocks you just created. Iron to fuse in place. Center a gold star on each of the red 8½" squares. Iron to fuse in place. Appliqué the edges of each shape with a narrow machine blanket stitch and matching thread.

Make 31.   Make 20.

Assembling the Quilt Top

1. Alternately sew together four Star blocks and three Christmas Tree blocks. Repeat to make a total of five rows.

Make 5.

2. Alternately sew together four Christmas Tree blocks and three plain ivory 8½" squares. Repeat to make a total of four rows.

Make 4.

3. Sew all the rows together to complete the quilt center.

4. Sew the green 4½"-wide strips together end to end to make one long piece. From this piece, cut two border strips, 72½" long, and two border strips, 64½" long. Sew the 72½"-long strips to the sides of the quilt. Sew the 64½"-long strips to the top and bottom of the quilt.

Finishing

Refer to "Quiltmaking Basics" on page 5 for detailed instructions on finishing techniques, if needed.

1. Piece the quilt backing so that it is 4" to 6" larger than your quilt top.

2. Layer the quilt top with batting and backing, and baste the layers together.

3. Quilt as desired and use the green strips to bind using your favorite method.

Finished Quilt Size: 64½" x 80½"

Finished Block Size: 8" x 8"

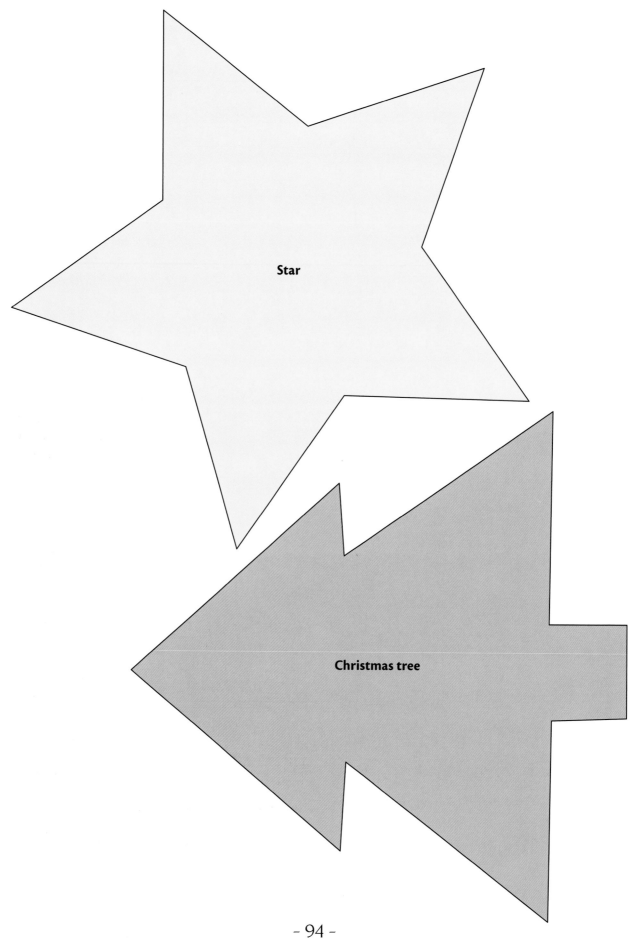

Star

Christmas tree

About the Authors

Quilt Designer and Author
Teri Christopherson

When Teri Christopherson was five years old, her mother sat her at the sewing machine and began what was to become a lifelong passion. By the time Teri was a teenager, she was spending all her spare change at the fabric store and sewing all her own clothes. She taught herself to quilt while in college, and a few years later as a young mother in search of a home business, she started her quilt-pattern business, Black Mountain Quilts.

As the mother of four children, Teri knows how hard it is to find time to quilt. She loves designing quilts that are quick and easy to make, yet still look impressive. She has designed hundreds of quilts and has authored more than 20 books and 30 patterns.

When she isn't quilting, Teri enjoys reading, throwing parties, and volunteering at church. She lives with her husband and four children near Mission Viejo, California.

Quilt Designer and Author
Barbara Brandeburg

Barbara Brandeburg has a vivid memory of her first trip to the fabric store with her mother as a young girl. Her heart raced and a passion for fabric and color was born. She has been designing and playing with both in one form or another ever since. She and her five sisters loved life around the sewing room with their sewing entrepreneur mother in a home filled with creativity and lots of girl gab time.

In the early nineties, Barbara and her sister Teri plunged into a fun adventure, sewing quilts to sell in boutiques in a darling little apple-and-antiques town called Julian, in Southern California. It was a natural next step to move onto pattern designing. Barbara launched Cabbage Rose with her first quilt designs and now has over 20 books, dozens of patterns, quilt fabrics, and giftware credited to her name. She gets a thrill out of the process of creating something better—usually a traditional theme with a new twist of trendy color and pattern.

While not designing, Barbara loves to garden, kayak, and take long river-trail walks in the woods. She and her husband John live near the rivers, lakes, and mountains of northern California. Their daughter Katie is away at college, while their son Travis serves in the army. Barbara's biggest new joy is her daughter-in-law Amber and grandson Hunter.

New and Bestselling Titles from

America's Best-Loved
Quilt Books®

America's Best-Loved Craft & Hobby Books®
America's Best-Loved Knitting Books®

APPLIQUÉ
Appliqué Quilt Revival—*NEW!*
Beautiful Blooms
Cutting-Garden Quilts
More Fabulous Flowers—*NEW!*
Sunbonnet Sue and Scottie Too

BABIES AND CHILDREN
Baby Wraps
Lickety-Split Quilts for Little Ones
The Little Box of Baby Quilts
Snuggle-and-Learn Quilts for Kids—*NEW!*
Sweet and Simple Baby Quilts

BEGINNER
Color for the Terrified Quilter
Happy Endings, Revised Edition
Let's Quilt!
Machine Appliqué for the Terrified Quilter
Your First Quilt Book (or it should be!)

GENERAL QUILTMAKING
Adventures in Circles—*NEW!*
Bits and Pieces
Charmed
Cool Girls Quilt
Country-Fresh Quilts—*NEW!*
Creating Your Perfect Quilting Space
Creative Quilt Collection Volume Three
A Dozen Roses
Follow-the-Line Quilting Designs
      Volume Three
Gathered from the Garden—*NEW!*
Points of View
Positively Postcards
Prairie Children and Their Quilts
Quilt Revival
A Quilter's Diary
Quilter's Happy Hour
Simple Seasons
Skinny Quilts and Table Runners
Twice Quilted
Young at Heart Quilts

HOLIDAY AND SEASONAL
Christmas with Artful Offerings
Christmas Quilts from Hopscotch—*NEW!*
Comfort and Joy
Holiday Wrappings—*NEW!*

HOOKED RUGS, NEEDLE FELTING, AND PUNCHNEEDLE
The Americana Collection
Miniature Punchneedle Embroidery
Needle-Felting Magic
Needle Felting with Cotton and Wool
Punchneedle Fun

PAPER PIECING
300 Paper-Pieced Quilt Blocks
A Year of Paper Piecing—*NEW!*
Paper-Pieced Mini Quilts
Show Me How to Paper Piece
Showstopping Quilts to Foundation Piece

PIECING
Copy Cat Quilts
Maple Leaf Quilts
Mosaic Picture Quilts
New Cuts for New Quilts
Nine by Nine
On-Point Quilts—*NEW!*
Ribbon Star Quilts
Rolling Along
Quiltastic Curves
Sew One and You're Done
Square Deal
Sudoku Quilts

QUICK QUILTS
40 Fabulous Quick-Cut Quilts
Instant Bargello—*NEW!*
Quilts on the Double
Sew Fun, So Colorful Quilts
Wonder Blocks

SCRAP QUILTS
Nickel Quilts
Save the Scraps
Simple Strategies for Scrap Quilts
Spotlight on Scraps

CRAFTS
Art from the Heart
The Beader's Handbook
Card Design
Creative Embellishments
Crochet for Beaders
Dolly Mama Beads—*NEW!*
Friendship Bracelets All Grown Up—*NEW!*
It's a Wrap
The Little Box of Beaded Bracelets
      and Earrings
Sculpted Threads
Sew Sentimental

KNITTING & CROCHET
365 Crochet Stitches a Year:
      Perpetual Calendar
365 Knitting Stitches a Year:
      Perpetual Calendar
A to Z of Knitting
Amigurumi World
Cable Confidence
Casual, Elegant Knits—*NEW!*
Chic Knits
Crocheted Pursenalities
First Knits
Gigi Knits...and Purls—*NEW!*
Kitty Knits
The Knitter's Book of Finishing Techniques
Knitting Circles around Socks
Knitting with Gigi
Modern Classics
More Sensational Knitted Socks
Pursenalities
Simple Gifts for Dog Lovers
Skein for Skein—*NEW!*

Our books are available at bookstores and your favorite craft, fabric, and yarn retailers. If you don't see the title you're looking for, visit us at www.martingale-pub.com or contact us at:

1-800-426-3126

International: 1-425-483-3313
Fax: 1-425-486-7596 • Email: info@martingale-pub.com

6/08